CW00340841

Misuse of Drugs

A STRAIGHTFORWARD GUIDE TO THE LAW

Misuse of Drugs
A Straightforward Guide to the Law
Leonard Jason-Lloyd

Published 2007 by
WATERSIDE PRESS
Sherfield Gables
Sherfield-on-Loddon
Hook RG27 0JG
United Kingdom

Telephone 01256 882250 UK Landline local-cost calls 0845 2300 733
E-mail enquiries@watersidepress.co.uk
Online catalogue and bookstore www.watersidepress.co.uk

Copyright © 2007 Leonard Jason-Lloyd. All rights are hereby reserved and have been asserted by the author in accordance with current UK and international legislation. No part of this book may be reproduced, stored in any retrieval system or transmitted in any form or by any means, including over the internet, without the prior permission of the publishers to whom copyright has been assigned for the purposes of this edition.

ISBN 9781904380320

Cataloguing-In-Publication Data A catalogue record for this book can be obtained from the British Library

Cover design Waterside Press.

Printing and binding Biddles Ltd, Kings Lynn, UK.

North American distributors International Specialised Book Services (ISBS), 920 NE 58th Ave, Suite 300, Portland, Oregon, 97213-3786, USA
Telephone 1 800 944 6190 Fax 1 503 280 8832 orders@isbs.com www.isbs.com

Misuse of Drugs

A STRAIGHTFORWARD GUIDE TO THE LAW

Leonard Jason-Lloyd

 **WATERSIDE** PRESS

Acknowledgements

My thanks go to Bryan Gibson for his painstaking attention to this book since it was originally introduced to him. I am also grateful to my wife, Usha, for her unfailing support and patience.

Leonard Jason-Lloyd

November 2006

CONTENTS

CHAPTER

APPENDIX

About the author

Leonard Jason-Lloyd has been a lecturer, accredited trainer and author for over 15 years. He has taught misuse of drugs courses to a very wide audience that includes university students, police officers, drug action teams, social workers, housing associations, solicitors, teachers, prison officers, probation officers, doctors, pharmacists, nurses, paramedics, and local authority employees. In addition to delivering numerous public broadcasts on TV and radio, he has also written many articles for law journals and over 20 books. He is a Fellow of the Royal Society of Arts, a Member of the Institute of Security Management, a visiting lecturer in criminal justice at the Midlands Centre for Criminology and Criminal Justice, Loughborough University and a visiting lecturer in medical law at the Department of Medical Sciences, University of Leicester. In addition to his academic work, he is also the proprietor of *Crime and Justice Consultancy and Training Service* where he delivers short courses on the law governing the misuse of drugs (email: lenjl@waitrose.com).

Acronyms, Abbreviations and Terminology
A Selection of Items Commonly Encountered

Controlled drug Controlled drugs fall under two main categories: (1) Medicinal drugs that cause social harm when misused; (2) Drugs of abuse that have no medicinal value and are only taken for recreational purposes. All controlled drugs are regulated by the MDA 1971 and its subordinate legislation, although those that have medicinal value are also regulated by the Medicines Act 1968.

Court of Appeal In terms of English domestic (or 'national') law, the Court of Appeal is the second highest court in the land, next only to the House of Lords (the 'Law Lords') although this court is due to be renamed the 'Supreme Court' from 2008. The Court of Appeal is divided into the Civil Division and the Criminal Division. It is the latter court in which the more important appeals concerning drug law are mainly brought. These involve cases initially decided in the Crown Court (see below), where convictions and/or sentences given in that court are disputed. The Court of Appeal (Criminal Division) has the power to overturn convictions or order retrials, as well as to modify or reduce sentences, where appropriate. Less frequently, this court may increase a sentence originally imposed by the Crown Court where the Attorney-General considers it to be excessively lenient and refers it to the Court of Appeal. Also, if a defendant has been acquitted of an offence in the Crown Court and this has arisen as a result of an unclear point of law, the Attorney-General may refer the anomaly to the Criminal Division of the Court of Appeal for a clarification of that law for future reference in similar cases.

Crown Court Generally, this court deals with the more serious criminal offences and, where applicable, the most serious crimes. The latter fall under the heading of 'offences triable only on indictment' which include all forms of homicide, robbery and rape. However, the Crown Court also deals with offences styled 'triable either way'. These may be tried summarily in the magistrates' court (below) or in the Crown Court, broadly depending on the wishes of the defendant or decisions by the magistrates. Generally, the Crown Court deals with the more serious triable either way offences where a conviction will attract a higher sentence than magistrates can impose (see further *Chapter 7*). The majority of crimes under the MDA 1971 are triable either way, therefore the venue of a trial is an important issue that has to be decided at an early stage of court proceedings for drugs offences. Nearly all trials in the Crown Court are conducted in the presence of a jury consisting of 12 ordinary citizens who decide on the guilt or innocence of the defendant. If he or she is found guilty, or pleads guilty, it is the Crown Court judge who presides over the court to then pass sentence.

Drug misuse This refers to drugs that are not administered in the correct manner or otherwise used to produce a non-therapeutic effect.

Hallucinogenic drug Controlled drugs that cause sights, sounds and other sensations that are not normally experienced in everyday life. This is known as 'taking a trip' as these experiences transport the drug user into a surreal psychological world. Sometimes these hallucinations take the form of living nightmares; on other occasions the opposite can occur. Drug users have no control over the effects of hallucinogens therefore serious psychological harm can be inflicted if the experience is traumatic. During 'trips' users of such drugs can also experience dangerous delusions such as being able to fly.

Magistrates' court The vast majority (as high as 97%) of all criminal cases are dealt with by magistrates' courts. Most drug offences are so dealt with as the majority of crimes under the MDA 1971 are classed as 'triable either way.' Unless the magistrates refuse to try the case because it is too serious or the defendant insists on his or her right to be tried before a jury, the case will be tried summarily before a bench of three lay magistrates (two in exceptional cases). Sometimes a district judge will sit alone and preside over certain cases. These are qualified lawyers who, unlike lay magistrates, are salaried and largely work full-time in the magistrates' courts. Whether a case is dealt with by lay magistrates or a district judge, both have the same sentencing powers which are more limited than those held by judges in the Crown Court (see, again, *Chapter 7*). This is often a crucial factor in determining whether someone charged with a triable either way offence is tried summarily before a magistrates' court or the Crown Court. In addition to having jurisdiction re either way offences, magistrates spend much of their time dealing with offences that are triable summarily only. These are mainly minor offences that can be dealt with relatively quickly.

MDA 1971 Misuse of Drugs Act 1971.

Medicines Act 1968 This statute and its subordinate legislation regulates all medicines available in England and Wales re their availability, production and overall safety. Not all medicines are controlled drugs. Those that are will also be regulated by the MDA 1971.

Medicines and Healthcare products Regulatory Agency (MHRA) Formerly the 'Medicines Control Agency', this body is linked to the Department of Health. The MHRA, among other things, acts as the watchdog re all medicines available in the UK and works under relevant provisions of the Medicines Act 1968 and its subordinate legislation.

Other misused substances A number of substances other than controlled drugs have caused concern for some years but, so far, have not been proscribed under the MDA 1971. One such range of substances are 'alkyl nitrites', known generally by the street name of 'poppers'. One of the better-known of these is 'amyl nitrite' that is regulated under the Medicines Act 1968 as it has limited medicinal uses and is available only on prescription. The fumes produced from these substances are inhaled in order to produce feelings of intoxication and sexual stimulation. Other substances that are inhaled in order to produce intoxication include certain solvents and gases whose sale and supply to young people is regulated under the Intoxicating Substances (Supply) Act 1985 and the Cigarette Lighter Refill (Safety) Regulations 1999 (SI 1999/1844). Finally, a shrub that grows in East Africa and surrounding areas known as 'Khat' is often the subject of debate re substance abuse. Although it contains the controlled drug 'Cathinone' (Class C, Schedule 1) which is a mild stimulant, the shrub itself is not controlled under the MDA 1971 even though the main method of ingesting the drug is by chewing its leaves. Recent investigations into the misuse of Khat have concluded that so far this does not amount to a significant threat as only a small section of the ethnic community are known to use this shrub and there is no evidence of more widespread usage.

Subordinate legislation The MDA 1971, and other statutes (or Acts of Parliament) are known as 'primary legislation'. However, Parliament also has the power to make 'subordinate' (or 'delegated') legislation, largely because certain statutes need to be flexible due to changing circumstances. The MDA 1971 is a good example as it concerns a very volatile aspect of human activity. In order to avoid having to constantly amend the MDA 1971, which can be a time-consuming process, there is provision for subordinate legislation to be made under this Act by ministers of state. This allows certain changes in the law to be made under a more streamlined procedure compared to that for amending a statute. The most well-known aspect of subordinate legislation under the MDA 1971 is its regulations, particularly those passed in 2001 which have been amended many times.

United Nations Treaties Three U.N. treaties govern the control of drugs in international law, namely the United Nations Single Convention on Narcotic Drugs 1961, the UN Convention on Psychotropic Substances 1971 and the UN Convention Against Illicit Traffic in Narcotic Drugs and Psychotropic Substances 1988. It is left to individual States, including the UK, to incorporate the obligations under these Conventions within their domestic (or 'national') law. The MDA 1971 is one such medium via which this is done.

World Health Organisation (WHO) A body which provides information on drug misuse to the United Nations Commission on Narcotic Drugs, as well as making recommendations.

The Purpose of this Book

Misuse of drugs has caused – and continues to cause - increasing concern in modern times but the law on this subject is quite complex. This book distils it into manageable portions with the aim of making it easier to understand. It untangles the complicated mix of legislation and case law that can make drugs law so difficult to understand, so as to provide a straightforward and basic guide for people who need an overview of the subject or simply to put matters into perspective, whatever their profession, vocation, interest or experience.

HOW THIS IS ACHIEVED

The book seeks to answer the following questions in particular:

- what are *controlled drugs*?
- why have they been given this name?
- what is the connection between *controlled drugs* and medicines?
- how have drugs been controlled in the past?
- what is the Misuse of Drugs Act 1971 and how does it function?
- what are 'the Regulations' under that Act and how do they work?
- what are the main drug offences?
- are there any notable defences to these crimes?
- what are the powers of the police and the courts when dealing with drug offenders?

It must be stressed that if legal advice is required in any specific case, this should be sought from an appropriate practitioner. This book is intended only as a practical introduction, not as a comprehensive source of law or practice in relation to the misuse of drugs. It should also be noted that changes to drug laws are a live issue and constantly being discussed – sometimes leading to amendment or revision; just as new approaches may be adopted by those drug workers in the community and in prisons. It is also important to note that the book applies to the law and legal system of England and Wales.

Recommended Further Reading

Emmett, D. and Nice, G. (2006), *Understanding Street Drugs*, 2nd Edition. London and Philadelphia: Jessica Kingsley Publishers.

Fortson, R (2005), *Misuse of Drugs: Offences, Confiscation and Money Laundering*, 5th Edition. London: Sweet & Maxwell.

Jason-Lloyd, L (2006), *Drugs, Addiction and the Law*, 11th Edition. Huntingdon: ELM Publications.

King, L. (2003), *The Misuse of Drugs Act: A Guide for Forensic Scientists*. Cambridge: Royal Society of Chemistry.

CHAPTER 1

What Are Controlled Drugs?

First of all, what is a drug? This is a word that can mean many things to different people. To some people it can mean a *medicine* to treat a particular illness or injury, whereas to others it can mean something to alter their senses for *recreational purposes*. According to the World Health Organization

> A drug is any substance taken into the body which alters the physical or psychological functions of the body.

The reason for taking a drug is therefore very important because this can often determine whether a drug is being used correctly or is being misused.

There are many hundreds of substances called 'drugs' or 'medicines'. All medicines in this country are regulated by the Medicines Act 1968 that is administered by the Medicines and Healthcare products Regulatory Agency (MHRA). Every medicinal product has to conform to certain requirements governing its production, availability and general safety. For instance, many medicines are available on prescription only; others are not - and may be purchased over the counter, but only from pharmacies and some of these may be packaged so as to contain a limited number of doses. Many other medicines are widely available on general sale without prescription from the shelves of supermarkets and other stores. But what are *controlled* drugs?

In the chart overleaf, on page 12 the large box symbolises all medicines that fall under the Medicines Act 1968. The smaller box in the top right-hand corner depicts drugs with medicinal properties but that fall under the Misuse of Drugs Act 1971 (MDA 1971) as well as the Medicines Act. These are called *controlled* drugs - because they come under the *double control* of both these Acts of Parliament. This is because controlled drugs can have particularly harmful effects when *misused*. When used correctly for medicinal purposes they should not be harmful, but when misused they can be addictive and/or may cause dangerous or bizarre behaviour.

These controlled drugs include diamorphine (medical heroin), cocaine, morphine, codeine, amphetamine, diazepam (valium) and many more. When such drugs are taken for the wrong reasons, harm can be caused to the individual concerned as well as to society as a whole.

Chart 1 *The difference between drugs and medicines*

The shaded box also depicts controlled drugs but these fall only under the Misuse of Drugs Act and not the Medicines Act as well. This is because they do not have recognised medicinal properties and are therefore just 'drugs' and not medicines. In other words, these are drugs that according to the law *can only be misused* and therefore cannot be safely prescribed. Examples include 'ecstasy', hallucinogenic drugs such as LSD, and nearly all forms of cannabis. These non-therapeutic substances have given rise to the saying that 'All medicines are drugs, but not all drugs are medicines!'

The full catalogue of controlled drugs appears in *Appendix 1* to this work, *List of Controlled Drugs.* Four things can be seen when that list is scrutinised (apart from the difficulty in pronouncing many names!):

- controlled drugs are placed into three classes, namely: A, B and C. This determines their perceived degree of dangerousness or social harm when misused. The most harmful fall into Class A, less dangerous drugs into Class B, followed by the least harmful drugs in Class C (as will be further explained later);

- the list does not merely contain a menu of individually named drugs (about 300 of them); it also includes numerous technical paragraphs describing an almost infinite number of chemical variations of these drugs, as well as defining chemical groups or families of drugs. It is therefore impossible to state accurately the exact number of known controlled drugs because of these variations; in other words, many drugs may yet be produced from these generic groups, and new variations may be discovered at any time;

- unless someone is well acquainted with chemical terms, it is unlikely that more than a few names will be familiar to them. One of the main reasons for this large number of unfamiliar drugs is that, in 1973, three controlled drugs were removed from the control of the MDA 1971, but had to be reinstated at a later date. These drugs were pemoline, phentermine and fencamfamin. As a result, not only is it now considered safer to keep redundant drugs on the controlled list in case their misuse is resurrected, but it is also necessary to retain them in order for the UK to comply with its international obligations (see the mention of three United Nations Conventions on page 19 of this work). So far, only two drugs have been permanently removed from the list of controlled drugs under the MDA 1971; these are prolintane (removed in 1973) and propylhexedrine (in 1995) (further mentioned on page 16); and

- a number in brackets is placed against each drug. This shows a further means by which each drug is categorised, namely the schedule it is placed under within the Misuse of Drugs Regulations 2001. This is explained in greater detail in *Chapter 3.*

CHAPTER 2

Misuse of Drugs Legislation

THE MISUSE OF DRUGS ACT 1971

The regulation of all controlled drugs falls mainly under the Misuse of Drugs Act 1971 (MDA 1971). This is a complex piece of legislation because it has to maintain a balance between allowing the *correct use* of certain controlled drugs at the same time as preventing their *misuse*. If all controlled drugs were just recreational and had no medicinal uses their regulation would be much easier because the MDA 1971 would simply outlaw all of them! This is not the case, and in order to achieve this balance, things sometimes become complicated.

Before looking at the MDA 1971, it is useful to examine the legislation that existed before 1971. In *Appendix 2* to this work, *The Development of Drug Legislation*, numerous provisions are listed relating to specific drugs that have been controlled over many years. But by 1971 there was so much drugs legislation that it was decided to control all drugs under one Act of Parliament, hence the MDA 1971. This consolidated all the previous law on controlled drugs and created some new offences. It also laid the foundations for all future controls over such drugs as well as new substances. In order to achieve all of its purposes, the MDA 1971 needed to be a flexible piece of legislation. *Appendix 3, Overview of the Misuse of Drugs Act 1971*, lists the main components of that Act. Some of these will not be covered in this book because they are of a highly specialised nature.[1] Provisions falling under the remaining sections are covered in various later chapters of this book.

Subordinate legislation under the Misuse of Drugs Act 1971

The chart on the opposite page depicts varieties of drug provision under the MDA 1971 *and its subordinate legislation*. It is this subordinate legislation that gives the 1971 Act its flexibility, otherwise it would need to be amended by Parliament every time even a minor change in the law was necessary - a cumbersome process that might take far too long. Instead, the MDA 1971 enables laws to be changed or made regarding controlled drugs, but without having to amend the Act itself. This is

---

[1]   Such as sections 11-17, 29, 30 and 32

achieved by allowing ministers of state to make subordinate legislation, called modification orders, designation orders or regulations. How do these work?

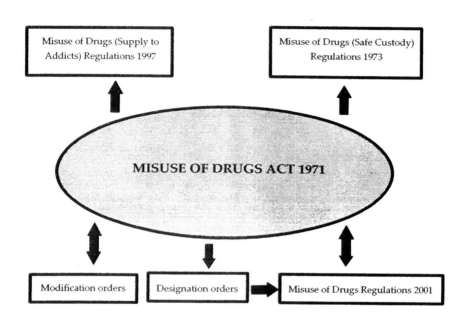

Chart 2 *The Misuse of Drugs Act 1971 and its subordinate legislation*

Modification orders
Modification orders are subordinate (or delegated) legislation through which new controlled drugs are placed under the control of the MDA 1971. They are also used to upgrade or downgrade controlled drugs that are already listed under that Act. It should be mentioned again at this stage that every controlled drug is placed under Class A, B or C, depending on the degree of dangerousness or social harm that the drug

can cause when misused. Sometimes it is necessary to change the classification of a drug if it proves to be more or less dangerous than originally believed. If this is the case, then a modification order is passed to change the class under which the drug is placed. On rare occasions modification orders have been passed to remove drugs from the controlled list completely.

A modification order is a statutory instrument that is laid before Parliament for a period of several weeks during which it can be scrutinised by both Houses of Parliament, Lords and Commons, and be amended by them if necessary. It is then enacted by The Queen (given 'royal assent') in the presence of about four Cabinet ministers (the Privy Council). This is known as an Order in Council. The whole process takes just weeks in comparison to at least several months to pass a new Act of Parliament.

Examples of modification orders include:

- the inclusion of anabolic/androgenic steroids as Class C controlled drugs in 1996;
- the reclassification of methaqualone from a Class C drug to Class B in 1984;
- the complete removal of propylhexedrine from the control of the Misuse of Drugs Act in 1995 (it was formerly a Class C drug); and
- the reclassification of cannabis and cannabis resin from Class B to Class C in 2004.

Designation orders

Designation orders are another form of subordinate legislation that can be made under the MDA 1971. Just as *modification* orders place new drugs under any of *three classes* of controlled drug, or upgrade, downgrade or remove them, *designation orders* are used to place new controlled drugs under any of the *five schedules in the Misuse of Drugs Regulations 2001*. They are also used to upgrade or downgrade existing controlled drugs from *one schedule to another*, or even to remove drugs from the schedules altogether. What are the schedules and what are the Misuse of Drugs Regulations 2001?

As mentioned above, every controlled drug is placed under Class A, B or C. At the same time each drug is placed under any of the five schedules under the Misuse of Drugs Regulations 2001. Again, *Appendix 1, List of Controlled Drugs,* depicts the *classes* under which each drug in that list has been placed and also the schedule that is shown in brackets alongside each substance. The schedules have been created so that therapeutic controlled drugs are not excessively restricted. This will be covered in more detail later. Note that Schedule 5 to the MDA 1971 is not mentioned against any of these drugs. This is because Schedule 5 is a miscellaneous schedule of various preparations that contain very small quantities of controlled drugs (see the final paragraph of *Appendix 5*, to this work, *Misuse of Drugs Regulations 2001, Schedules 1-5*).

The Misuse of Drugs Regulations 2001 that contain the five schedules are themselves another aspect of subordinate legislation passed under the authority of the MDA 1971. This is because these regulations contain many other provisions enabling the correct use of controlled drugs and items related to them. These will become more apparent as this book unfolds.

Designation orders are made in much the same way as modification orders except that they are ultimately passed by Parliament before being sent for royal assent rather than just by The Queen in the presence of the Privy Council. They also take just several weeks to become law and often run in tandem with modification orders. Some examples of designation orders are as follows:

- the upgrading of temazepam from Schedule 4 to Schedule 3 in 1995;
- the upgrading of flunitrazepam from Schedule 4 to Schedule 3 in 1998; and
- the complete removal of propylhexedrine from the control of the MDA 1971 and its regulations (it was formerly under Schedule 4). Note that this occurred in tandem with the modification order mentioned above regarding the same drug.

The Misuse of Drugs Regulations 2001
As mentioned above, the Misuse of Drugs Regulations 2001 contain many provisions that enable the correct use of controlled drugs and related matters. Examples include the issuing of licences to lawfully produce controlled drugs or to approve the use of specific premises for cannabis growing for *research purposes*, the supervision of the destruction of controlled drugs, and the marking of bottles and other containers, record keeping requirements (from many more). Also, as mentioned above, the Misuse of Drugs Regulations 2001 contain the five schedules under which all controlled drugs are placed. Other regulations that exist under the MDA 1971 are noted in what follows.

The Misuse of Drugs (Supply to Addicts) Regulations 1997
These enable (only) specially authorised doctors to prescribe certain controlled drugs to *addicts*. These drugs are cocaine, diamorphine and dipipanone. However, doctors who are not so licensed may prescribe these drugs, but only for the treatment of disease or injury and not for addiction.

The Misuse of Drugs (Safe Custody) Regulations 1973
Certain premises where controlled drugs are kept have to conform to these regulations in order to ensure the safety and general security of these substances. In order to avoid them falling into the wrong hands, the regulations cover a number of detailed provisions concerning where and how controlled drugs are to be stored. These include certain minimum standards regarding the types of cabinets and safes that may be used as well as the structure of the rooms where drugs are housed.

OTHER MISUSE OF DRUGS LEGISLATION

The MDA 1971 and its subordinate legislation does not work in isolation. There are a number of Acts of Parliament passed since 1971 that operate in conjunction with it to effect controls over 'controlled substances'. Again, *Appendix 2, The Development of Drug Legislation* notes and describes some of the primary legislation that has worked alongside the MDA 1971 since its enactment.

OTHER MECHANISMS

The Advisory Council On The Misuse Of Drugs
Appendix 3, Overview of the Misuse of Drugs Act 1971, mentions Section 1 and schedule 1 of the MDA 1971 making provision regarding the Advisory Council on the Misuse of Drugs (ACMD) that is central to the workings of the 1971 Act and its subordinate legislation. The MDA 1971 states that there must be at least 20 members of the ACMD although, in practice, it normally numbers about 35. This body has a duty to advise the Government on all aspects of the misuse of drugs, and the Home Secretary must first consult with the ACMD before making any changes to misuse of drugs legislation. It also has the power to initiate research on drug misuse. It has a wide membership that includes doctors, dentists, veterinary practitioners, pharmacists, non-pharmaceutical

chemists, a judge, a teacher, experts in social problems connected with the misuse of drugs, as well as chief police officers, to name but a few.

International obligations

UK drug laws are often influenced by its obligations to give effect to the recommendations of the United Nations Commission on Narcotic Drugs, which in turn acts on the advice of the World Health Organization. This is because the UK is a party to two UN Drug Conventions, namely the United Nations Single Convention on Narcotic Drugs 1961 and the three United Nations Conventions, namely the UN Single Convention on Narcotic Drugs 1961, the UN Convention on Psychotropic Substances 1971 and the UN Convention Against Illicit Traffic in Narcotic Drugs and Psychotropic Substances 1988. As noted earlier on page 13, another reason why so many redundant substances remain listed under the MDA 1971 is that they are still retained under these UN Conventions.

CHAPTER 3

Unlawful Possession

As mentioned in *Chapter 2*, the Misuse of Drugs Act 1971, and its subordinate legislation, endeavours to create a balance between preserving the *correct use* of controlled drugs whilst making rules that prevent their *misuse*. This has made the law complex, and as far as the *possession* of controlled drugs is concerned this is not always a straightforward matter. There are three main reasons for this:

- many patients would be deprived of the medicinal properties of certain controlled drugs if the legal rules were too restrictive;
- if the legal rules were not restrictive enough, many would take advantage and misuse these drugs even more; and
- the MDA 1971 does not define the meaning of 'possession', so that guidance has to be obtained from the case law (or 'precedent') as this has built up over the years. This will be summarised below under 'A Checklist on Unlawful Possession'.

The main source of the law that prohibits the possession of controlled drugs is section 5(1) and (2) of the MDA 1971. Apart from some specific defences that will be discussed later, the provisions state that 'it shall not be lawful for a person to have a controlled drug in his possession.' Of course, there are many exceptions to what would otherwise be an absolute rule, or else every doctor, dentist, veterinary practitioner, nurse, pharmacist and many other people who possess controlled drugs for good reason, would be committing a criminal offence every time they did so, e.g. in order to relieve suffering. Can you imagine what would happen if morphine, for instance, was completely banned? In order to allow the correct use of controlled drugs, there are many exceptions to the general prohibition as outlined below.

A CHECKLIST ON UNLAWFUL POSSESSION

1. Is the substance a controlled drug?
This may seem obvious, but an important step in proving whether a person was in possession of a controlled drug is to provide evidence that

the substance was, in fact, a controlled substance. For instance, it could be another substance that is not controlled or prohibited in any way. So how is this proved?

- First, by forensic science analysis, although note that the MDA 1971 does not state the minimum quantity of a drug that is necessary to secure a conviction. What is the legal situation where a minute quantity of a drug is found, such as scrapings of heroin or traces of cannabis in the bowl of a pipe? A defendant will not be guilty of possession of a controlled drug if the prosecution cannot prove that the defendant knew of its existence. This will apply if the quantity of the drug is so small that the defendant could not have known of its presence. In 1982, in *R v. Boyesen*[1] the court ruled that the presence of the drug must at least be visible before the defendant can be convicted. Earlier cases were decided on whether the quantity of the drug was too small to be used. Now the test is whether the presence of the drug was detectable by the person concerned. However, even possession of a tiny quantity of drugs could be evidence of past possession in certain circumstances. Each case is judged on its own merits.

- Secondly, is the substance a controlled drug? Again, this may seem an obvious question, but many tablets and other preparations are not necessarily controlled drugs, although they may fall under the Medicines Act as noted in *Chapter 1*. If the substance *is* a controlled drug then it will be found under Schedule 2 to MDA 1971 (see *Appendix 1* to this work, *List of Controlled Drugs*).

WHAT IS POSSESSION?

As mentioned above, the MDA 1971 does not provide a definition of possession. This has to be gleaned from case law that has built up over many years. The general rule is that possession means the defendant had physical custody or control of the substance plus knowledge of its existence, nature and quality. In the case of nearly all criminal offences there must be a guilty act or conduct (called an *actus reus* under the criminal law), and there must also be a guilty mind (known as *mens rea*). Physical custody or control of the drug is the *actus reus* and knowledge

---

[1] *R v. Boyesen* [1982] AC 768

of its existence, nature and quality is the *mens rea*. What is physical custody or control?

Physical custody of drugs

An example of physical *custody* is where drugs are found on a person such as in their pockets or in a bag or parcel that they are carrying. If not actually on the person, how close do the drugs have to be to amount to physical custody? The answer can be found in case law, although do not expect the law to be always clear-cut. The judges decide cases on their own merits and even those that are similar do not always produce the same outcome. For example, in *Feeney v. Jessop* (1990)[2] the accused was found lying next to a radiator over which a towel was draped that had a piece of cannabis on top of it. Although he admitted ownership of the towel to the police he would not say anything else. The court held that he was in possession of the cannabis because of the location of the drug and that he had the power to remove it from the towel.

But contrast that case with the earlier decision in *Tansley v. Painter* (1969)[3] where two people were in a car and one of them was selling drugs from the vehicle. The court held that the person who was not selling the drugs was not guilty of being in joint possession of them. This was because he had mere knowledge of the other person selling drugs and this did not amount to having control of them. It is worth noting that in similar circumstances there could be a charge of aiding and abetting a drug offence. However, it must then be proved that the other party was providing some encouragement or assistance either actively or passively. But just mere knowledge of what was happening is still not enough for a conviction.

Physical control of drugs

Physical *control* is different in so far as the drugs need only be accessible to the defendant and not necessarily close by. One example is where someone conceals a packet containing controlled drugs in a safe deposit box and keeps the key. Because that person has control over the drugs, they will be in his or her possession even if that person travels hundreds of miles away. In either case, what is the legal position if the defendant is not aware that a container such as a packet, parcel or bag contains controlled drugs? In such cases, there may be a defence under section 28 of the MDA 1971. This is covered separately below together with other

---

[2] *Feeney v. Jessop* [1990] SCCR 565 HCJ Appeal
[3] *Tansley v. Painter* [1969] Crim LR 139

special defences to charges regarding the unlawful possession of controlled drugs.

Possession of drugs in shared accommodation
How does the law affect people in jointly occupied premises who share accommodation with others? Again, each case is judged on its own merits and we have to look at case law for guidance. For example, in *Hughes v Guild* (1990)[4] two people lived together in a house of which they were the sole occupiers. In the living room, the police found two open packets of cigarette papers, two pieces of cannabis, and a knife was lying nearby that contained traces of the drug. The court held that both were guilty of unlawfully possessing cannabis because (1) these items were lying openly in their own living room and (2) they were able to do as they wished with the drugs because they were the only people living there. In other words, each of them had sufficient knowledge and control of the drugs to convict them of unlawful possession. But contrast this decision with *R v Smith* (1966).[5] In this case, the accused was arrested in a house that was occupied by other residents. In one of the rooms that was in common use by the other residents, the police discovered a form of cannabis. The court held that the arrested person only had a general interest in that room and this was not sufficient to convict that person.

The importance of 'knowledge'
The above are just two selected cases that give some insight into the different circumstances regarding the possession of controlled drugs. In this instance they are concerned with drugs found in premises that are occupied by more than one person. Once again, the key elements are whether someone has sufficient knowledge of the existence of the drugs and control over them. But an interesting question is sometimes asked regarding 'knowledge' of the existence of a drug,.i.e. 'If a person says he or she forgot they had the drug in their possession; does this mean that they have a defence because they did not have any knowledge of the drug's existence when arrested?' This could be especially problematic if there was evidence that the drugs were originally possessed a considerable time earlier. In *R v. Martindale* (1986)[6] someone took possession of some cannabis when in Canada. Two years later this was found in his wallet by the police in the UK. He admitted that he put it

---

[4] *Hughes v. Guild* [1990] JC 359
[5] *R v. Smith* [1966] Crim LR 588 CA
[6] *R v. Martindale* [1986] 84 Cr App R 31

there but had completely forgotten it. The court held that possession did not depend on the accused person's memory, otherwise the law would favour those with poor memories against those who had good memories.

At this stage it is important to mention that there is a separate offence of *allowing* certain drug offences to take place on premises, rather than *possessing* the drugs concerned. This is covered by section 8 of the MDA and is discussed under *Chapter 6*.

IS THE PERSON ONE OF THOSE EXEMPT BY THE 2001 REGULATIONS?

Note that we are now dealing with the Misuse of Drugs *Regulations* 2001 and *not* the MDA 1971. In other words we are now concentrating on some of the subordinate or secondary legislation made under the Act itself as explained in *Chapter 1*. By way of a reminder, the Misuse of Drugs *Act* creates the main prohibitions regarding controlled drugs, whereas the Misuse of Drugs *Regulations* 2001 concentrate mainly on the exceptions to many of those prohibitions. This is designed to prevent the misuse of controlled drugs as much as possible but without impeding the therapeutic use of these substances. In effect, this is a balancing exercise between the Act itself and the regulations made under it. Examples of how this works follow below within the descriptions of people who are exempt under the regulations.

People licensed by the Home Office

Under Regulation 5 of the Misuse of Drugs Regulations 2001, people licensed by the Home Office may possess, produce, supply or offer to supply any controlled drug. Needless to say, there will have to be good reasons for applying for such a licence, for example, research by a recognised institution such as a university. The licence will specify the drug in question and certain conditions may be attached to the use of that drug including about where it is to be kept. Regulation 5 states that:

> Where any person is authorised by a licence of the Secretary of State issued under this regulation and for the time being in force to produce, supply, offer to supply or have in his possession any controlled drug, it shall not by virtue of section 4(1) or 5(1) of the Act be unlawful for that person to produce, supply, offer to supply or have in his possession that drug in accordance with the terms of the licence and in compliance with any conditions attached to the licence.

If anyone deviates from the conditions of such a licence, as where he or she takes drugs home to show friends and family, that is an offence under section 18 MDA 1971. This offence of licence contravention is triable either way, meaning that it can be tried either before magistrates (summarily) or before a judge and jury in the Crown Court (on indictment). When tried on indictment in the Crown Court, the maximum sentence is two years' imprisonment and/or an unlimited fine (see *Appendix 4* to this work, *Maximum Penalties for Drug Offences*, for the list of other offences under the MDA 1971 and their maximum penalties as they currently stand.)

People with general authority to possess (and supply) *any* controlled drug
Regulation 6(7) of the Misuse of Drugs Regulations 2001 states that the following persons may lawfully possess any controlled drug, and may supply that drug to any person who may lawfully receive it. Note this applies to *all* controlled drugs, whether or not they have medicinal properties.

'(a) A constable acting in the course of his duty as such'
Note that the precise wording refers to a 'constable' meaning a police officer of any rank, including special constables, as well as officers within the Serious Organised Crime Agency (SOCA) provided they have been designated as such. This does not apply to police auxiliaries, such as community support officers (CSOs), as they do not hold the office of constable, but have been given a range of powers for specific situations as described in *Chapter 8.* The word constable also refers to prison officers within HM Prison Service who have the powers of a constable when on duty, but this does not extend to prisoner custody officers working in privately managed prisons or with the prisoner escort service that, e.g. takes prisoners to and from court to a prison. They may rely on other powers that will be mentioned later. It is important that someone holding the office of constable who possesses a controlled drug, is acting in the course of his or her duty at the time, otherwise that officer will be outside of the legal protection of this regulation.

It should be emphasised that Regulation 6(7) states that once the above people have taken possession of a controlled drug, they may then only supply it to someone who may lawfully receive it. For example, a police (or customs) officer who has seized a controlled drug in the course of their duty, would be acting outside the protection of this regulation if that officer gave the drug to someone other than a person who is lawfully entitled to receive it. Authorised persons will, for instance, include other such officers.

'(b) A person engaged in the business of a carrier when acting in the course of that business'
Increasingly, private carriers are used to transport controlled drugs to many legitimate destinations including hospitals as well as other places such as forensic science laboratories and pharmacies. Of course, such an organization may be required to prove that they are legitimately operating as a carrier, otherwise criminal elements would use this as an excuse for being in possession of controlled drugs. Any person who possesses a controlled drug who relies on this exemption, must be acting *within the scope of that business*. Thus, for instance, if a driver working for a private carrier happens to be caught in possession of 'ecstasy' tablets for personal consumption, that driver has some explaining to do!

'(c) A person engaged in the business of the Post Office when acting in the course of that business'
This is really self-explanatory. In addition to private carriers, the Post Office also conveys controlled drugs to many legitimate recipients. As mentioned under the previous item above, the possessor of the drugs must be acting within the course of that business and must supply (or deliver) those drugs to persons lawfully entitled to receive them such as hospitals and pharmacies. In other words a diversion of those drugs into the wrong hands will form the basis of a criminal offence as this will place the possessor outside the protection of the regulations.

'(d) An officer of customs and excise when acting in the course of his duty as such'
It is obvious that customs and excise officers (now part of Revenue and Customs) who, e.g. seize drugs at ports and airports, must, in the same way as the police, have legal immunity re their legitimate actions, otherwise they would not be able to perform many important duties in dealing with core aspects of illegal drug activities such as importation and exportation. Again, such officers must be acting in the course of their duty - as with those who hold the office of constable. Also, certain officers within SOCA may be designated with customs officer powers.

'(e) A person engaged in the work of any laboratory to which the drug has been sent for forensic examination when acting in the course of his duty [when] *so engaged'*
Certain laboratories are authorised to carry out the forensic examination of substances in order to ascertain whether they are controlled drugs.

People working in such laboratories may possess any controlled drug provided they are legitimately engaged in work of this nature. If, for instance, a person working in such a laboratory is caught smoking cannabis, that person also has some explaining to do!

It should be mentioned again that Regulation 6(7) states that once the above people have taken possession of a controlled drug, they may then only supply it to someone who may lawfully receive it. A police or customs officer who possesses a controlled drug in the course of his or her duty, would be acting outside the protection of this regulation if that officer gives the drug to someone other than a person who is entitled to receive it. In the case of laboratory staff, private carriers and Post Office employees, they too must not pass on controlled drugs to others unless the latter are legitimate recipients, and where this is part of their official duties of both parties.

'(f) A person engaged in conveying the drug to a person who may lawfully have that drug in his possession'
A prime example of this legal immunity would include someone collecting a prescribed controlled drug from a pharmacy on behalf of a patient who is too ill to do this for himself or herself. However, if the collector of that drug diverts from his or her route and takes it to someone who is not lawfully entitled to possess it, this places that person outside the protection of this regulation.

Drugs *legitimately* prescribed
So why in view of all the above is the word 'legitimately' stressed or even mentioned at all? 'Surely', an observer might ask, 'if a drug has been obtained on prescription then no offence can be committed?' But this may not always be the case.

Regulation 10 to the Misuse of Drugs Regulations 2001 states, among other things, that a person must not make a false statement in order to obtain a controlled drug on prescription. If they do, they may then be in possession of it unlawfully. Examples include: someone deliberately lying to a doctor claiming that they are severely stressed in order to obtain a mild sedative such as diazepam (valium), but then using this drug to obtain a 'high'; or someone falsely claiming that they are in severe pain in order to obtain a painkiller such as dihydrocodeine (DF118), but later using it to create a state of euphoria. In other words, controlled drugs obtained on prescription should only be used for their proper purpose. Anything other than this places the possessor of the drug outside the protection of Regulation 10 and makes the possession unlawful.

A case that illustrates this point is *R v Dunbar* (1981)[7] where a doctor possessed heroin and pethidine obtained on prescription, intending to use these to commit suicide. The court held that the doctor was guilty of unlawfully possessing these drugs because they were taken for a non-medicinal purpose and thus he fell outside the scope of Regulation 10.

Regulation 10 also prohibits a practice known as 'double scripting'. This occurs when someone obtains a prescription from a doctor but later obtains more drugs from another medical practitioner without telling that second doctor about the first prescription. A person obtaining a second (or additional) supply of drugs by the use of deceit, will be in unlawful possession of them.

PEOPLE EXEMPT UNDER SCHEDULES 1 TO 5 OF THE 2001 REGULATIONS

The Misuse of Drugs Regulations 2001 contain over 25 pages of rules and exemptions regarding various aspects of matters relating to controlled drugs. In many ways these regulations fill in some of the gaps left by the MDA 1971. Apart from those specifically mentioned elsewhere in this book, these provisions cover such matters as the destruction of drugs, the marking of bottles and containers, record keeping requirements, forms of prescriptions and much more. A highly important aspect of these regulations, as stated earlier, is the inclusion of five schedules. Every controlled drug (or generic family or chemical variation), is not only placed under Class A, B or C under the Misuse of Drugs Act, but also under a schedule to the Misuse of Drugs Regulations 2001. Again, *Appendix 1* to this work, *List of Controlled Drugs,* shows the *class* under which each drug is placed under the MDA 1971, and then against each named drug is the number that denotes the *schedule* it appears under within the 2001 Regulations. *Appendix 5, Misuse of Drugs Regulations 2001, Schedules 1-5,* lists the people who may lawfully possess (and supply) controlled drugs.

It may be useful to look at *Appendix 1* and *Appendix 5* in conjunction with *Chart 2* in *Chapter 2* in order to appreciate the overall picture as to

---

[7] *R v. Dunbar* [1981] 1 WLR 1536

how the MDA 1971 and the Misuse of Drugs Regulations 2001 work together and interact; then the 'balancing exercise' between the two also becomes clearer. The meaning of section 5(1) MDA 1971 will also come into focus:

> **5.** (1) Subject to any regulations under section 7 of this Act for the time being in force, it shall not be lawful for a person to have a controlled drug in his possession.

The 'regulations under section 7' include the Misuse of Drugs Regulations 2001 that make many of the exceptions to the rule that 'it shall not be lawful for a person to have a controlled drug in his possession.' A number of other exceptions have already been outlined above but more follow below.

IS THE PERSON EXEMPT UNDER THE MDA 1971?

A number of exemptions are also provided to certain people under the MDA 1971 itself. These appear within sections 5(4) and 28 of that Act.

Section 5(4) of the Misuse of Drugs Act

Section 5(4) MDA 1971 provides two separate lines of defence to certain people who have good reasons for taking possession of any controlled drug. The first of these, under section 5(4)(a), applies to people who take possession of a controlled drug in order to prevent another person from committing an offence in connection with that drug. This will apply, for instance, where a person finds what he or she knows or suspects to be a controlled drug and takes temporary possession of it to stop someone else from misusing the drug. The person who intervenes in this way will have a defence provided that they take reasonable steps as soon as possible to either destroy the drug or to deliver it to someone who is lawfully entitled to take custody of it, such as a police officer.

One class of person who may use this power could include prisoner custody officers (PCOs). As mentioned earlier in this chapter, PCOs are *not* prison officers employed by HM Prison Service (HMPS), but they perform security duties in privately managed prisons and/or within the prisoner escort service. Unlike their HMPS counterparts they do not have the powers of a constable when on duty. They may therefore rely on section 5(4)(a) in order prevent drug misuse, including drug dealing, among prisoners. This defence may also apply to parents who confiscate drugs from their children and either destroy the drugs or deliver them up to the police, or any other persons lawfully entitled to receive them; and similarly to teachers or youth justice workers.

The second line of defence comes under section 5(4)(b). It applies where someone knows or suspects that a substance is a controlled drug and in order to deliver it to someone lawfully entitled to possess it, he or she takes reasonable steps to do this as soon as possible. This is not contingent on preventing a crime in connection with a controlled drug and does not require it to be destroyed. This might apply, e.g. to people who take unused prescription drugs back to a pharmacy or to a doctor.

Section 28 of the Misuse of Drugs Act 1971
Before explaining section 28, it is important to re-state that possession of a controlled drug means physical custody or control, plus *knowledge* (see earlier in this chapter). If there is a lack of knowledge, then a person may have a defence if he or she is accused of a drugs offence; although this will depend on whether the defendant raises the issue which the prosecutor cannot disprove. Section 28 MDA 1971 can provide a defence if there is a lack of knowledge where:

- the defendant did not know, suspect or have reason to suspect that he or she had *any* drug in his or her possession.

   Example A street drug dealer is spotted by the police, so he quickly slips a packet of crack cocaine into the bag of an innocent passer-by, intending to retrieve it later. If that passer-by did not know what happened, then he or she will not have any awareness of the packet or indeed of any drug being in his or her possession.

- the defendant was aware that they possessed a drug but did not know, suspect or have reason to suspect that the substance was a *controlled drug*.

   Example Someone innocently picks up a bottle that is labelled 'aspirin' but is unaware that it really contains heroin. Although that person knows of the existence of the substance, he or she is not aware that it is heroin.

- the defendant was aware that he or she possessed a controlled drug but did not know, suspect or have reason to suspect that it was a category of controlled drug that he or she is prohibited from having.

> **Example** Someone obtains a prescription for diazepam (a Class C drug), but due to a mistake at the pharmacy the bottle is filled with methadone (a Class A drug). Although that person knows that he or she is in possession of a controlled drug, they are not aware that it is methadone that normally they would not be allowed to have.

Questions of fact

The defendant's knowledge or suspicions are judged by magistrates or juries who have to be convinced of their validity. In other words the more credible and believable the defence, the more likely it is to succeed. However, the burden of proving guilt falls on the prosecutor, therefore if magistrates or juries are left with reasonable doubt regarding knowledge of suspicions, the defendant must be acquitted.

Defences under section 28 MDA 1971 do not apply to all drug offences. The offences where this defence can apply include: possession, possession with intent to supply, producing or manufacturing, supplying or offering to supply, cultivating cannabis, opium-related offences, and ships used in the illicit trafficking of controlled drugs.

SPECIAL AND GENERAL DEFENCES

Thus far this chapter has looked at *specific* (often called 'special') defences to various offences under the MDA 1971. It is also important to examine the *general* defences that exist under the wider criminal law and that can apply across a whole range of other crimes – as well as drug offences. Not all general defences may apply to the misuse of drugs, although most do. This will be examined in the next chapter.

CHAPTER 4

General Defences

Apart from those specific or 'special' defences that have been written into the Misuse of Drugs Act 1971 and the Misuse of Drugs Regulations 2001 as discussed in *Chapter 3*, it is also necessary to consider the role of the general criminal law in providing defences to drug related offences. The key general defences that are likely to be in issue are noted below. Generally speaking, once the accused raises sufficient evidence in support of a general defence the onus remains with the prosecutor to disprove it as part of his or her case against the accused – and to the criminal standard of proof, beyond reasonable doubt.

INTOXICATION

The rules governing intoxication as a defence under the general criminal law are quite complex. As far as drug offences are concerned, a useful guideline can be found in *R v. Young* (1984)[1] where the defendant was caught selling LSD whilst he was drunk. As his intoxication was self-induced (voluntary) he had no defence. However, if the intoxication is involuntary, the defendant may have a defence if they were unable to form the necessary criminal intent, for instance. Involuntary intoxication includes situations where a person may be forced into taking an intoxicating substance or is tricked into taking it, as where his or her drink is laced or 'spiked'. This may also include a person who becomes intoxicated on prescribed medication, provided that person does not misuse the prescribed medicine, such as by exceeding the prescribed dosage or mixing it with another drug or alcohol.

INFANCY

Infancy in this context means that a person is below the age of criminal responsibility. In England and Wales the age of criminal responsibility is ten years of age. Therefore, if a child commits a drug offence, or indeed

---

[1] *R v. Young* [1984] 1 WLR 654

any other criminal act, and is below that age, he or she cannot be prosecuted. This does not mean that the authorities can do nothing whatsoever when this occurs as there are a number of powers under the civil law where such youngsters may be kept under care or supervision, or referred to various agencies (or 'services') with a view to some kind of intervention with regard to themselves and/or their parents. Offenders who have reached the age of ten but are under 18 years are usually dealt with differently under that part of the criminal justice system known as the youth justice system. For instance, the vast majority of them appear before the youth court instead of any of the adult criminal courts. Also, the sentencing regime for young offenders is different in so far as special disposals apply to them such as referral orders, supervision orders and action plan orders. Much of this work is done through local youth justice teams (or YOTs). Sometimes the parents or guardians of young offenders may be ordered to play a part in preventing their re-offending.

INSANITY

This is a very controversial aspect of the criminal law as legal insanity can be very different from its clinical counterpart. This is because the rules governing insanity under the criminal law were formulated as far back as 1860, although this has been subject to a great deal of interpretation by the judges since then. Legal insanity is broadly defined as a disease of the mind that causes such a defect of reason that the defendant is either completely unaware of his or her actions, or was aware but did not know that they were wrong. This definition falls under what are called the M'Naghten Rules.[2]

If someone is charged with a drug offence and had a severe mental defect that falls under these rules, then it is possible that this could provide a defence. However, legal insanity only provides a partial defence or a special verdict, and not an outright acquittal. The special verdict of 'not guilty by reason of insanity' restricts the courts to a limited list of disposals rather than the full range of sentences normally available for offenders. Some of these do not involve any form of custody although the latter will apply where the offender is dangerous. Despite reforms of the law governing the insanity procedure, this special verdict tends to be avoided due to the stigma of being found legally insane.

---

[2] *M'Naghten's Case* [1843-60] All ER 229

In cases where legal insanity is not put forward as a defence, evidence of mental disorder may lead to other disposals available to the courts. These include hospital orders or guardianship orders that can be imposed under the Mental Health Act 1983, or a community sentence with a requirement for psychiatric treatment under the Criminal Justice Act 2003. Also, various schemes have been piloted in different parts of the country where defendants apparently suffering from mental disorder are examined by doctors before appearing in court. If a doctor is satisfied that a defendant could be treated and the necessary facilities are available, this can avoid a criminal trial. However, the general shortage of facilities for treating the mentally impaired is often an obstacle in dealing with such people in this manner. Despite the procedures for dealing with them, a large proportion of people are given custodial sentences who suffer from mental health problems. Many of these are wholly or partly drug-related which has become a central issue concerning the appropriateness of the use of prisons or young offender institutions for such people, especially given the rising prison populations and overcrowding.

DURESS BY THREATS

This is a general defence that is increasingly put forward by defendants charged with drug and other offences. Under certain circumstances, this defence can lead to an outright acquittal if the defendant was forced to commit a drug offence because they were threatened with immediate death or serious injury. This may also apply if someone else was placed in imminent danger as shown by *R v M* (2003).[3] In that case, a woman convicted of drug smuggling gave evidence that she lived in Jamaica with her young daughter and a sick elderly mother. She went on to state that she was approached by a man who offered to pay for her mother's medical treatment provided she smuggled drugs into the UK. She initially refused, but then her mother's condition worsened and so she had reluctantly agreed to go through with it when the man returned, but later changed her mind. The man then threatened to kill her, as well as her mother and daughter if she ran away. She was later abducted by him and another man causing her to fear for her life. Over £90,000 worth of cocaine was concealed on her and she was then taken to an airport and told that she would be watched constantly. She also stated that she did not inform customs officers or the police on her arrival in the UK because

---

[3] *R v. M* [2003] Sol J 420. CA (Crim Div)

she thought that they were in league with the man who made the threats. Her conviction for unlawfully importing cocaine was overturned by the Court of Appeal because insufficient guidance had been given to the jury. That court stated that the test of the defence of duress by threats involves the following three questions that could have usefully been put to the jury in that case:

(1) Did the defendant believe there was a real possibility of at least serious harm being inflicted on herself, or to her daughter or mother, unless she committed the offence?
(2) Would an ordinary person of reasonable firmness, sharing the characteristics of the defendant, have reacted in the same way?
(3) Could the defendant have escaped or avoided the threat without endangering herself or her relatives, which a reasonable person would have taken in a similar situation?

Several cases have reached the Court of Appeal in modern times where drug addicts have become indebted to drug dealers and have been forced into committing crimes, whether drug offences or other crimes, under threat of death or serious injury. This is an increasing problem as many drug dealers have a reputation for making such threats and sometimes they carry them out. Not surprisingly perhaps, the judges of the Court of Appeal have stated that those who become indebted to drug dealers place themselves in 'a bad position'. The following cases illustrate this fact very clearly.

In *R v. Harmer* (2001)[4] the defendant, a drug addict, was convicted of smuggling 1.2 kilogrammes of pure cocaine into the UK. Although he put forward the defence that he committed this crime under the threat of violence, the Court of Appeal dismissed his appeal against conviction. The court held that becoming indebted to a drugs supplier was a voluntary act so that he had exposed himself to unlawful violence, and this could not be used as an excuse for the crime he committed.

The defence of duress by threats was put forward in the earlier case of *R v Heath* (1999),[5] where the defendant was a heroin addict who owed £1,500 to a drug dealer. This debt was then transferred from the dealer to someone with a reputation for violence that was known to the defendant. In order to reduce the debt by £1,000 he agreed to drive a large quantity of cannabis across the country. He was caught and

---

[4] *R v. Harmer* [2001] Crim LR 401
[5] *R v. Heath* [1999] Crim LR 109

convicted of possession of a (then) Class B drug with intent to supply. The Court of Appeal refused to overturn his conviction on the grounds that he had voluntarily exposed himself to unlawful violence by becoming indebted to a drug dealer and that he had had more than one opportunity to escape. The judgment in this case was followed by that of the Court of Appeal in *R v Harmer* above.

Rather different facts were put forward in *R v Ali* (1994)[6] although this case still involved becoming indebted to a drug dealer. Here, the defendant was an addict who sold drugs but his dealer agreed to let him keep enough for himself. On one occasion, however, the defendant used all the drugs himself and therefore owed money to the dealer who had a reputation for being very violent. The dealer threatened to kill the defendant unless he repaid the debt by committing an armed robbery using a gun given to him by the dealer. The court ruled that a person who voluntarily takes part in criminal offences such as drug dealing with anyone known to be violent and likely to demand that criminal offences be committed, cannot rely on the defence of duress.

In the more recent case, that of *R v Hasan* (2005),[7] the House of Lords significantly restricted the circumstances under which the defence of duress may be used. This defence will not apply if the following conditions exist:

- the defendant failed to contact the police even though there was the opportunity to do so.;
- the defendant should have realised that the people he associated with might put him under pressure to commit a crime; and
- the threat of death or serious injury was not reasonably believed and genuinely held by the defendant.

There are occasions when the defence of duress may not succeed as a complete defence but may be used to reduce the sentence in appropriate circumstances. An example is *R v Taonis* (1974)[8] where the defendant was forced to smuggle cannabis into the UK because of a threat to beat and torture the woman he was living with. Also, the defendant himself was threatened with false accusations that he had committed a serious theft. His appeal against conviction did not succeed on the grounds that there was an interval during which he could have notified the police.

---

[6] *R v. Ali* [1995] Crim LR 303 CA
[7] *R v. Hasan* [2005] UKHL 22 [2005] All ER (D) 299 (Mar)
[8] *R v. Taonis* [1974] 59 Cr App R 160

However, the Court of Appeal recognised that he had been subjected to a terrifying ordeal and reduced his sentence from four years' imprisonment to two years.

NECESSITY (DURESS OF CIRCUMSTANCES)

The defence of necessity (or 'duress of circumstances' as it is often known) basically means that the accused may be acquitted of certain criminal charges if he or she acted in an emergency or other extreme situation. There has been a build up of case law over many years where people have been absolved from criminal liability when they have committed criminal acts but in extreme circumstances such as saving life and limb, either their own or others. In effect, the defendant is choosing the lesser of two evils. It is possible that this may be used as a defence to certain charges of drug offences where the defendant found himself or herself in a life or death situation for instance, although each case is judged on its own facts. However, in *R v. Huckell* (1998)[9] the Court of Appeal stated that this defence was not available in cases where a drug is unlawfully possessed in order to treat a medical condition (although it is interesting to note that juries have in practice been known to acquit defendants in such cases). In *R v. Quayle, Wales, Kenny, Taylor and Lee* and *Attorney General's Reference (No.2 of 2005)*,[10] the Court of Appeal made it clear that the defence of necessity does not apply to anyone who possesses cannabis or cannabis resin with intent to supply it, even if that person intended to supply the drug to another in order to reduce their pain arising from an illness such as multiple sclerosis. In effect, this would enable unqualified persons to prescribe cannabis to themselves or others. This point was also made in the more recent case of *R v. Altham* (2006)[11] concerning the possession of cannabis for pain relief.

OTHER POSSIBILITIES

Under the general law there is a defence of 'mistake of fact', i.e. where the accused claims to have believed the facts to be other than they actually are. Where someone has taken drugs, drink or a combination of

---

[9] *R v. Huckell* [1998] EWCA Crim 3365
[10] *R v. Quayle, Wales, Kenny, Taylor and Lee* [2005] EWCA Crim.1415 CA (Crim Div)
[11] *R v. Altham* [2006] EWCA (Crim) 7

both their perceptions may become blurred and the former law on what occurred became somewhat complicated. With regard to drug-taking, mistake of fact is now covered under section 28 MDA 1971 (above); and readers may also find it useful to consider see *Haggard v Mason* on page 41. There are also situations where drugs become part and parcel of an argument whether the accused was able to form the *mens rea* for a particular offence and what effect this may have in a given situation; but such matters are better studied as part of criminal law in general rather that a book on the law relating to misuse of drugs as they often involve broader principles or knowledge of elements of given offences. It is sufficient to note and be aware of such interplay.

CHAPTER 5

Unlawful Supply

POSSESSION WITH INTENT TO SUPPLY

Before examining the unlawful supply of controlled drugs, it is important to look at an offence that was created by the Misuse of Drugs Act 1971, section 5(3). This is the offence of *possession with intent to supply*. Section 5(3) makes it unlawful for someone to possess a controlled drug if they have the intention to supply it to another person who is not lawfully entitled to receive it. It makes no difference whether the person is in possession of the drug lawfully or otherwise. Therefore, for instance, if someone has been legitimately prescribed a drug but intends to give or sell it to someone else who is not lawfully entitled to possess it (see *Chapter 3*), the offence of possession with intent to supply will be committed by the person who so acts. It makes no difference whether or not payment is to be made for the drug.

The intention of the defendant is, of course, crucial in such cases and this is often proved by surrounding circumstances and the general conduct of that person as well as any admissions made by him or her. Thus, e.g. substantial quantities of drugs may constitute evidence of the intention to supply them, although this may not always apply as addicts often build up their own stocks of drugs with no intention of passing them on to anyone else. It should be noted that section 2 of the Drugs Act 2005 makes provision for the courts to presume that there was the intention to supply a drug if more than a specified amount of that drug was in the defendant's possession. However, the government announced in October 2006 that it will not put this law in force, for the time being at least. This was due to a lack of consensus on the part of those involved in the consultation process regarding the national threshold as to the amount of drugs that a person could possess without being charged with possession with intent to supply.

Possession of a controlled drug with intent to supply is classed as a drug trafficking offence (see *Appendix 4* to this work, *Maximum Penalties for Drug Offences*). An example of this offence can be seen in *R v Moore*

(1979)[1] where the defendant prepared a cannabis joint for smoking and intended to share it with two other people. It was held by the court that the defendant committed the offence of possession with intent to supply. What is the legal position where a cannabis joint is passed around during a party? The perpetrator who commences the distribution will normally be guilty of supplying the drug, and as the 'joint' is passed around, each recipient will be guilty of possession but not possession with intent to supply. This is because each recipient will only have temporary control of the drug that is destined to be returned in diminished size to the original distributor.

Sometimes, people caught possessing controlled drugs unlawfully, try to escape conviction for that offence by claiming that they were merely holding them for someone else. This could backfire because that person could then be convicted of the more serious offence of possession with intent to supply. This can be seen from *R v. Maginnis* (1987),[2] where the defendant alleged that cannabis found in his car had been left there by his friend who was going to collect the drugs later. The House of Lords held that he was guilty of possession with intent to supply the cannabis because he was going to return the drugs to his friend.

UNLAWFUL SUPPLY OF CONTROLLED DRUGS

Section 4(1) MDA 1971 states that it is an offence to produce, supply, or offer to supply a controlled drug to another person. This is subject to any defences under section 28 MDA 1971 and others as mentioned in *Chapters 3* and *4*, as well as in *Appendix 5, Misuse of Drugs Regulations 2001, Schedules 1 to 5*. The Misuse of Drugs Regulations 2001 also provide legal protection to any patient who has been prescribed a controlled drug and returns it (namely supplies it) to the person from whom he or she obtained the drug, such as their doctor or pharmacist. The regulations overlap to a certain extent by also allowing the patient, or person acting on his or her behalf, to return a prescribed controlled drug to any doctor, dentist or pharmacist for destruction. It should also be noted that controlled drugs may be prescribed by vets in order to treat animals. The regulations also allow people to return such drugs to any vet or pharmacist for the purposes of destruction.

---

[1] *R v. Moore* [1979] Crim LR 78
[2] *R v. Maginnis* [1987] AC 303

Section 4(1) of the Misuse of Drugs Act does not state that a person unlawfully supplying a controlled drug must also be in unlawful possession of it in the first place; and it is submitted that it is, indeed, irrelevant whether the drug is unlawfully possessed by the supplier or not. The offence is supplying or offering to supply the drug to someone who is not lawfully entitled to receive it, whether the drug has been legitimately obtained or received through the illicit market. This is in line with the offence of possession with intent to supply.

Another legal point that is sometimes raised is, 'What happens if a substance offered as a controlled drug turns out to be something different?' Say, for instance, a someone is offered cocaine when in fact the substance is aspirin. The person making the bogus offer will still be guilty of offering to supply cocaine. This principle is illustrated in *Haggard v Mason* (1976)[3] where the defendant bought some tablets believing them to be LSD and then sold some of these to a third party who also believed the same. The tablets, in fact, did not contain any controlled substance, but despite this mistaken belief, the defendant was convicted of offering to supply a controlled drug. This is one instance where section 28 of the MDA 1971 does not apply.

Also, if for instance cocaine (Class A) is offered to someone when the substance is amphetamine (Class B), the person making the offer will be guilty of offering to supply cocaine.

Deaths arising from the supply of drugs

Anyone who administers a controlled drug is regarded as supplying that drug, unless that person is merely assisting the drug user. If A injects B with heroin, then A is guilty of supplying the heroin. A will not be guilty of supplying the drug if he or she is merely assisting in its administration. However, the situation becomes more complex where a drug is unlawfully supplied to a person who subsequently dies as a result of taking it. This is because it becomes a manslaughter (or possibly even a murder depending on the accused person's intentions) case and is subject to the general criminal law regarding who is criminally liable for the victim's death. Although a number of cases have been decided on this issue, there is still a degree of uncertainty. This is due to the courts stating that the link between the supplier and the victim's death, must still be decided by the jury. Some cases have ruled that a supplier is not guilty of manslaughter if he or she merely encourages the victim to take

---

[3] *Haggard v. Mason* [1976] 1 W.L.R. 187

the drug. In the case of *R v. Rogers* (2003),[4] the Court of Appeal upheld the defendant's conviction for manslaughter and administering poison so as to endanger life, because the defendant actually took part in the injection of heroin by holding a tourniquet around the victim's arm. In *R v. Kennedy* (2005),[5] the defendant prepared a syringe containing heroin for someone else who then injected himself with the drug and died within the hour. In this instance, the defendant prepared the drug for administration to the victim rather than just supplying it. The Court of Appeal held that it was open to the jury to convict the defendant of manslaughter if the conduct of the victim and the defendant was a 'combined operation' consisting of one activity, namely administering the heroin.

UNLAWFUL SUPPLY OF DRUG KITS AND DRUG PARAPHERNALIA

'Drug paraphernalia' consists of items that can be used to unlawfully administer or prepare controlled drugs. Examples include tubes, knives, razor blades, metal foil, matches, clay pipes and many others. These are usually 'normal' items that can be supplied for a range of legitimate purposes but they can also be used in the unlawful administration and preparation of controlled drugs. Also, drug kits have been sold that contain a collection of such items. Section 9A MDA 1971 makes it an offence to supply or offer to supply any article that can be used to unlawfully prepare or administer a controlled drug for misuse by anyone. This also applies where the article is adapted for this purpose either for use by itself or in combination with something else. There is no such offence as merely being in 'possession of prohibited drug paraphernalia,' but see below regarding the specific offences of possessing utensils for the preparation of opium and its smoking, although these only apply to that drug. Also, in order to protect people who believe they are innocently supplying such items for legitimate purposes, there must be evidence that the supplier of a prohibited article believed that it was to be used in the unlawful administration or preparation of a controlled drug.

---

[4] *R v. Rogers* [2003] EWCA Crim. 945
[5] *R v. Kennedy* [2005] EWCA Crim 685

LAWFUL SUPPLY OF DRUG PARAPHERNALIA

Further harm reduction measures were later introduced by extending section 9A MDA 1971. As a result of these changes, specified people who include doctors, pharmacists and authorised drug workers may supply certain drug paraphernalia to drug misusers. The items that may be supplied are: sterile water ampoules, swabs, ascorbic acid, filters, citric acid and mixing utensils such as bowls. It is important to note that these are the only forms of drug paraphernalia that may be supplied by authorised persons. Therefore supplying or offering to supply articles such as tourniquets, for instance, is still unlawful under section 9A of the 1971 Act. Drug workers have been warned to be careful if supplying any ready-made drug kits in case they contain one or more of the prohibited articles that fall outside the recent changes in the law.

It is not an offence under section 9A to supply or 'offer to supply hypodermic syringes or their needles. This is a well-known harm reduction measure both in prison and in the community where the practice is sometimes called 'needle exchange' and is designed to reduce the spread of serious diseases such as the HIV virus that are often associated with the use of contaminated needles and syringes. Even if hypodermic syringes and their needles are supplied by people who are less than respectable, an offence will not be committed under section 9A.

OPIUM OFFENCES

Section 9 of the MDA 1971 has created the following offences in connection with opium:

- to smoke or otherwise use prepared opium;
- to frequent opium dens;
- to possess utensils such as pipes, used or intended for the smoking of opium; and
- to possess utensils used for the preparation of opium for smoking.

In view of the serious problems that were once associated with opium smoking, these prohibitions remain under misuse of drugs legislation. In modern times there appears to be evidence that this historic form of drug misuse may be returning, although it remains to be seen to what extent it is likely to be of serious concern. Section 9 is subject to the special defences under section 28 of MDA 1971 as described in *Chapter 3*.

It is interesting to note that the first part of section 9, namely the offence of smoking or otherwise using prepared opium, is the only offence under the MDA 1971 where the actual *use* of a controlled drug is a crime.

CHAPTER 6

Drug Activities on Premises

Section 8 of the Misuse of Drugs Act 1971 is headed: 'Occupiers etc. of premises to be punishable for permitting certain activities to take place there'. Many drug-related activities occur on premises, therefore this aspect of the MDA 1971 is intended to compel certain people to self-police those places, in order to prevent or stop a range of drug offences occurring there. The essential ingredients of this offence are as follows (the key elements being written in italics):

A person commits an offence if they are the *occupier* of *premises* or concerned in their *management*, and *permits or suffers* the following activities to take place there:

- unlawfully producing or attempting to produce a controlled drug;
- unlawfully supplying or attempting to supply a controlled drug;
- unlawfully offering to supply a controlled drug;
- preparing opium for smoking; or
- smoking cannabis, cannabis resin or prepared opium.

The MDA 1971 does not define the key terms in section 8 namely, 'premises', 'occupier', 'management', 'permit' or 'suffer'. Instead, guidance has to be gleaned from case law that has developed over many years as outlined below.

WHAT IS MEANT BY 'PREMISES'?

Although some precise definitions of 'premises' have been decided under case law, there are certain instances where this is open to question. Those that are certain include buildings, certain objects and appliances that are part of land, enclosed open land such as backyards, gardens and alleys, moored ships and houseboats, and pleasure boats. Other legislation, namely the Police and Criminal Evidence Act 1984 (or PACE) and the Private Security Industry Act 2001, collectively state that premises include vehicles, aircraft, hovercraft, offshore installations, as well as tents or moveable structures. It is up to the judges in any future cases to decide whether any of the latter fall within section 8 MDA 1971.

WHO MAY BE LIABLE UNDER SECTION 8?

Section 8 states that it is a person who is the 'occupier' or is concerned 'in the management' of any premises that may be liable for permitting or suffering certain drug-related activities. Although it is for the courts to decide if someone falls under any of these headings, much depends upon that person's power to exclude drug misusers from the premises. They may or may not necessarily be the owner of the premises as it depends on their degree of control over them. Other people who are potentially liable can include tenants, managers or anyone who exercises control over the premises. The following cases have provided some guidance as to who this includes.

R v. Tao (1977)[1]
This is the leading case on deciding who is the occupier for the purposes of section 8. In this instance, the defendant lived in a student hostel where he rented a room to which he had his own key. He was the sole occupier of this room where he ate, slept, washed and studied. During a search, the police found evidence of a drug gathering having been held in the defendant's room namely discarded cannabis joints, including one that was still smouldering at the time. In this case the defendant was held to have been the occupier and therefore liable under section 8.

R v. Coid (1997)[2]
The defendant was convicted of permitting or suffering premises to be used for the unlawful supply of cannabis. His girlfriend was the tenant of the flat where this occurred, although the defendant was looking after the premises while she was away on holiday. In his defence he claimed that he was not the occupier of the flat but the court held that his girlfriend's tenancy did not preclude him from being the occupier, and he was therefore liable under section 8.

R v. Ashdown (1974)[3]
In this case, four people were convicted of allowing each other to smoke cannabis in premises where they were all co-tenants. The Court of Appeal upheld their convictions on the grounds that a co-occupier who permits or suffers another co-occupier to commit prohibited drug

---

[1] *R v. Tao* [1977] QB 141
[2] *R v. Coid* [1998] Crim LR 199 CA
[3] *R v. Ashdown* [1974] 59 Cr App R 193 CA (Crim Div)

activities on premises, is also liable under section 8, just as if the co-occupier had invited a friend into the premises and permitted them to commit the unlawful act. However, the Court of Appeal did not state the degree of control that a co-tenant would be expected to exert on another where the prohibited act was being committed.

R v. Josephs (1977)[4]

Even people occupying premises unlawfully may be liable under section 8. In this case the defendant was a squatter in a basement where he ran a card school and where there was evidence of cannabis smoking as well.

R v. Souter (1971)[5]

The defendant let rooms in his house to drug addicts. He placed a notice on his door stating that the police would be called if anyone brought drugs into the premises. However, evidence of drugs was found but his conviction was overturned on the grounds that he had taken reasonable steps to prevent the drug activity. There was also evidence that on more than one occasion he had excluded people who were carrying drugs.

WHAT IS 'PERMITTING' OR 'SUFFERING'?

In most cases the twin formula 'permits or suffers' conveys a single meaning. Collectively the term means turning a blind eye to or ignoring the prohibited drug activity and doing little or nothing to stop it. However, there must be actual knowledge that this is occurring and not mere suspicion. Examples of this can be seen in the following two cases.

In *R v. Thomas and Thomson* (1976)[6] one of the defendants allowed his friend, a seaman, to stay in his house when on shore leave. The police entered his home and found cannabis and cannabis smoking equipment that he stated belonged to his friend. He then said, 'I have asked him not to smoke in my house but what can you do? He is a good mate and I could not kick him out'. The court held that he did little to prevent cannabis being smoked on the premises and that knowledge of what was happening included turning a blind eye to the obvious.

In *R v. Brock and Wyner* (2000)[7] both defendants (also known as 'The Cambridge Two') managed a day centre for the homeless and each was

---

[4] *R v. Josephs* [1977] 65 Cr App R 253
[5] *R v. Souter* [1971] 1 WLR 1187
[6] *R v. Thomas and Thomson* [1976] 63 Cr App R 65
[7] *R v. Brock and Wyner* [2001] 1 WLR 1159

convicted for having taken insufficient steps to prevent heroin dealing on the premises. For about two years, the police told them that substantial heroin dealing was taking place at the centre. The defendants banned some of the drug dealers from the premises although this was more limited than the figures conveyed to the police; they also refused to disclose the names of those people. In their defence they stated that they had a policy of confidentiality that would have been breached if they disclosed the names of those banned from the centre. Also, they had limited numbers of staff on the premises and feared reprisals from the dealers if they gave the latter's names to the police. Their convictions under section 8 were upheld by the Court of Appeal although their original prison sentences were substantially reduced.

GAPS IN SECTION 8

An examination of section 8 of the MDA 1971 discloses some obvious omissions. Among other things, it does not include smoking 'crack' cocaine, neither does it mention injecting or smoking heroin nor sniffing cocaine, to name but a few drugs. This attracted criticism for a number of years and eventually an attempt was made to resolve this anomaly. The government inserted an amendment to section 8 through the medium of the Criminal Justice and Police Act 2001 that was progressing through Parliament at the time. This amendment significantly extended the scope of section 8 by including the administration or use of any controlled drug which was unlawfully in a person's possession at the time or immediately beforehand. Although this was sometimes called 'the crack house amendment,' it went much further as it was a catch-all provision that would have sealed-up the gaps in section 8. However, due to the wide nature of this provision, the government promised that it would not be put into force unless there had been extensive consultation. This process invoked strong opposition from a number of factions, especially people working in harm reduction schemes who felt that they would be especially vulnerable to prosecution. It was reported that to some extent, the case of the Cambridge Two (see *R v Brock and Wyner* above) had sent out a warning signal that was exacerbated by the proposed amendment to section 8. Despite numerous attempts to introduce safeguards in order to make drug workers less vulnerable, this amendment was eventually repealed and section 8 remains as originally enacted. Instead, an alternative strategy was devised under the Anti-social Behaviour Act

2003 whereby 'crack houses' in particular are targeted rather than drug offenders. This will be discussed below.

POLICE POWERS TO CLOSE 'CRACK HOUSES'

Part 1 of the Anti-social Behaviour Act 2003 gave to the police extensive powers to close down so-called 'crack houses', i.e. places where 'crack' cocaine is used, produced or supplied. In addition to the individual and wider social harm inflicted by the misuse of this drug, these places have gained notoriety for the serious disruption and degradation they cause to local communities in their vicinity.

Basically, the police may initially prohibit *public* access to such premises for up to 48 hours during which magistrates will consider issuing an order for the complete closure of those premises *to everybody* for up to three months. If this is granted, the premises will be boarded up for the duration of the order and in certain circumstances this may be extended for up to a further three months.

Anyone who defies or obstructs these closure powers commits a criminal offence. These powers also apply to any premises where other Class A drugs are unlawfully used, produced or supplied. The closure powers must only be used where the illegal drug activities are also causing serious disruption to the local community. Officers from the Serious Organized Crime Agency (SOCA) may also exercise the powers of closure under the 2003 Act, although they must be designated for this purpose and be given police powers accordingly. It is interesting to note that the forthcoming reclassification of methylamphetamine from Class B to Class A will, among other things, give the police the same powers to close premises used to unlawfully use, produce or supply this drug, as apply to 'crack' houses (see *Chapter 10*).

Since 2003 there have been a number of high profile closures including of premises in the West End of London and one of the UK's foremost discotheques in Brixton, South London. In many ways these closure powers have been very effective, but in some cases this may only apply in the short term. There is the possibility that closing such places may merely displace the problems rather than address them at their root source. The dealers may simply relocate to other premises as they are unlikely to give up their activities in view of the potentially massive financial gains attributable to their illicit trade.

Although the government's strategy is to focus on premises rather than people found there, the police have the option also to make arrests where appropriate.

CHAPTER 7

Incitement, Attempt and Conspiracy

Under the criminal law, incitement, attempt and conspiracy are collectively called 'inchoate' offences. These are offences that fall short of the complete (or substantive) offence in contemplation, and that is why they are also sometimes called 'preliminary offences' (as opposed to the 'ultimate', 'intended' or 'substantive' offence that is in mind). These offences apply in connection with the majority of controlled drugs offences as they do across the remainder of criminal conduct and may sometimes be of particular relevance in this area of the law, including, e.g. where third parties are involved in the drug chain, such as 'street dealers' and 'drug mules', or where a delivery fails to reach its destination because it is intercepted. It is necessary to regard such activities as crimes in order to target (and some people argue to deter) criminal acts at every stage, whether or not the ultimate or substantive offence is actually committed.

INCITEMENT

Although incitement under the general criminal law is governed by the common law (case law), section 19 of the Misuse of Drugs Act 1971 specifically relates this to the misuse of drugs and states:

> It is an offence for a person to incite another to commit such an offence.

This offence of incitement occurs when someone encourages, persuades, pressurises or threatens one or more people to commit a crime. It does not matter if those others refuse to take part, the crime of incitement will still have been committed by the person doing the incitement. Therefore, if a drug dealer incites several people to sell drugs on the street, he or she will be guilty of incitement to unlawfully supply drugs even if all the intended street dealers refuse to take part.

What if the intended offence cannot be fulfilled?
Incitement may still be committed even if circumstances make it impossible for the substantive offence to be carried out, although this

usually applies if the incitement to commit a crime is not too specific. An example could include a drug dealer asking someone to help unload a consignment of drugs from a lorry and says that he or she will give that other person further details later, but unknown to the dealer the lorry has already been taken off the road. The principle of impossibility also applies to the two other inchoate offences of attempt and conspiracy noted below.

ATTEMPT

A criminal attempt occurs where someone intends to commit an offence (the *mens rea*) and does an act which goes beyond merely preparing to commit it (the *actus reus*).[1] A major problem often encountered in proving criminal attempts is the dividing line between the preparatory stages of an intended crime and the actual attempt stage. The decision as to whether an attempt has been made is a question of fact that is left to the jury, magistrates or the district judge in an individual case. The principal source of the law governing attempts is the Criminal Attempts Act 1981. Since 1981, a number of cases have been decided where the judges have been asked to interpret that Act in the context of specific cases, one of which is discussed below.

What if the attempted offence is impossible to commit?
As well as in certain cases of incitement (above), the defence of impossibility does not apply to criminal attempts or conspiracies either. A useful illustration of this principle can be seen in *R v. Shivpuri* (1987)[2] where the defendant was caught importing a suitcase that he expected to contain heroin and confessed to this when arrested. However, customs officers had substituted a harmless vegetable substance beforehand (a process known as a 'clean delivery' when carrying out certain anti-drug operations). Despite his mistaken belief, the defendant was convicted of attempting to import heroin.

Certain crimes cannot be attempted from the outset, namely offences that are triable summarily only, unless there is a legal provision that states otherwise in specific cases. However, this issue is unlikely to arise as nearly all offences under the MDA 1971 fall under the higher classification of triable either way (i.e. triable either before magistrates

---

[1] The broad nature of *actus reus* and *mens rea* is explained in *Chapter 1*.
[2] *R v. Shivpuri* [1987] AC 1

or in the Crown Court depending on a procedure known as 'mode of trial' or 'determining venue' that takes place in the magistrates' court).

CONSPIRACY

Nearly all conspiracy offences are covered by the Criminal Law Act 1977, including those concerning drug related crimes. If two or more people agree to participate in a crime and then plan the intended offence, this will constitute a conspiracy to commit it. Even if one or more parties to a conspiracy have no intention of taking part in all of the agreed conduct, as long as they agree to an unlawful object and intend to play at least some part in the agreed conduct, they will be guilty of conspiracy. This is shown by *R v. El Ghazal* (1985)[3] where the defendant organized a meeting between two people so as to arrange a deal regarding cocaine during which he was present for only a short space of time. All three were later charged with conspiracy to obtain cocaine. The defendant's conviction was upheld on the grounds that he brought the other two conspirators together, knowing that at least one of them would try and obtain cocaine.

Where drug offences have been committed by a number of people but it is not clear as to the precise part that each played in the enterprise, it is quite common for each participant to also be charged with conspiracy to commit that offence; thus increasing the chances of a conviction where such people might otherwise escape liability.

Is anyone exempt from conspiracy?
It is not usually an offence for someone to plan a crime completely on their own. But if this is done in combination with one or more other people, then it will constitute a crime. But certain people may not be criminally liable for a conspiracy. These include victims of the conspiracy, the spouse of a conspirator provided the husband and wife are the only participants to the conspiracy, or someone under ten years of age (i.e. below the age of criminal responsibility anyway). But this will not mean that a co-conspirator escapes liability. He or she can be convicted even if the other conspirator(s) are exempt.

---

[3] *R v. El Ghazal* [1986] Crim LR 52 CA

What if the intended offence cannot be committed?

Even if the intended offence is impossible to fulfil, the offence of conspiracy to commit that offence will still be committed. An example can be seen in *R v. Harris* (1979)[4] where the defendant and others intended to unlawfully produce amphetamine. Although this was impossible because they had the wrong ingredients and did not completely understand the correct production method, they were still convicted of conspiring to produce a controlled drug.

Drug conspiracies committed abroad

If two or more persons conspire in Germany (or elsewhere abroad) to import drugs into England, they can be tried for conspiracy in this country whether or not the intended offence actually occurred. Also, the reverse can apply, provided the conspiracy that takes place in this country concerns a proposed drugs offence that is against the law in the intended country abroad as well as here.

A similar law exists under section 20 MDA 1971 that states:

> A person commits an offence if in the United Kingdom he assists in or induces the commission in any place outside the United Kingdom of an offence punishable under the provisions of a corresponding law in force in that place.

The above can be illustrated by *R v Vickers* (1975)[5] where the defendant made an agreement in England to collect some speaker cabinets in which cannabis was later concealed, load the speakers onto a truck that he obtained in London, and then take them to Italy, which he later did. The cannabis was then destined to be shipped to the USA. The defendant was convicted of conspiracy to contravene section 20 of the 1971 Act because of his agreement to assist in or induce the commission of an offence in the USA that was against a corresponding law in the UK. The court held that by virtue of the defendant collecting the speakers and obtaining the truck in the UK, there was enough evidence of 'assistance' on his part in the UK to convict him.

---

[4] *R v. Harris* [1979] 69 Cr App R (Crim Div)
[5] *R v. Vickers* [1975] 1 WLR 811

CHAPTER 8

Police Enforcement Powers

The police are increasingly used to combat the misuse of drugs on several fronts. This includes education programmes in schools, for instance, as well as their vital role in enforcing the law. Although the police service is the biggest and most visible of all law-enforcement bodies, it is certainly not the only one. The others include HM Revenue and Customs, the Serious Organized Crime Agency (SOCA) and the Assets Recovery Agency. Between these agencies and in some instances other partner organizations from the Criminal Justice System it is now, but only quite recently, possible to seriously disrupt the activities of people involved in the world of illegal drug production or supply and in some cases before or irrespective of an arrest or successful prosecution.

The main focus of this chapter is on the powers of the police because of their more visible day to day role in combating drug misuse in an enforcement capacity. The two main sources of police powers in this context are the Misuse of Drugs Act 1971 and the Police and Criminal Evidence Act 1984 (or PACE). The statutory powers covered in this chapter will be confined to the searching of people, vehicles and premises for controlled drugs and the arrest of drug suspects.

POLICE POWERS TO SEARCH PEOPLE AND VEHICLES FOR DRUGS

Section 23(2) MDA 1971 states that a police officer may do the following if that officer has reasonable grounds to suspect that any person is in unlawful possession of a controlled drug:

- detain and search that person;

- stop any vehicle or vessel in which the police officer suspects that the drug may be found; and

- seize and detain anything found during a search which appears to be evidence of an offence under the MDA 1971.

Two important matters need to be explained at this stage. The first is the meaning of the term 'reasonable grounds to suspect;' the second relates to the way the police should conduct searches for drugs.

'Reasonable grounds to suspect'

A police officer's suspicion should be based on the guidance outlined in the Codes of Practice that work in conjunction with PACE. Among many other things, these codes state that this suspicion must be based on objective factors such as specific information (sometimes called 'intelligence') or a suspect's conduct; for example, a someone who is obviously trying to conceal something. This may also be linked to the time of day (or night) and the place, such as an area well known for drug dealing especially at given times. Suspicion must not be solely based on subjective or personal factors such as someone's race, religion, appearance or known criminal past. However, people associated with groups or gangs that are known to habitually carry controlled drugs (and weapons), may be searched. This applies if they wear distinctive clothing or insignias such as tattoos, that identify them with the group, although this information must be based on reliable police information.

Conduct of police searches

Section 2 of PACE in conjunction with the Codes of Practice sets out the rules governing the conduct of searches by the police. The main elements are as follows:

- the police officer should inform the suspect that he or she (or the vehicle) are being detained in order to be searched;

- the police officer should state his or her name and the police station where he or she is based (the officer may not give their name if they believe it might put them in danger, but may give their warrant number instead). If the officer is not in uniform he or she must produce his or her warrant card;

- the suspect must be told the legal search power being used;

- the police officer should clearly explain the purpose of the search (to find drugs for instance) and the grounds for the search, namely what made the officer suspicious;

- where a search of a person is made in a public place such as the street, the search must not go beyond a superficial examination of outer clothing. This is often confined to a 'frisk' or 'pat down', although a police officer may feel inside pockets, collars, socks and shoes. The suspect must not be required to remove more than an outer coat, jacket or gloves in public. If it is necessary for more clothing to be removed, this must be done out of public view such as in a police van or at a nearby police station;

- if a search is required that will expose *intimate* parts of the body, this must not be done in a police vehicle. Instead, this should be done at a nearby police station or nearby location out of public view;

- an arrested suspect may be subjected to an *intimate* search for a controlled substance only if it is a Class A drug that is reasonably believed to be concealed in any of the body orifices, namely the anus, vagina, nose or ears (the searching of mouths is not regarded as an intimate search). Intimate searches must be authorised by a police officer of at least the rank of inspector and should be carried out by a doctor or nurse in medical premises. The search may only take place if the suspect consents to it, but in the event of a refusal without good reason, an adverse inference may be drawn if the case goes to court. In other words, 'did the suspect have something to hide?';

- if an arrested suspect is believed to have swallowed any Class A drug, a police officer of the rank of inspector or above may authorise an X-ray and/or ultrasound scan. Either or both may only be taken on medical premises by a doctor or nurse. The suspect's consent to this procedure must be given, although if this is refused without good reason, an adverse inference may be drawn if the case comes before the court;

- apart from the specific rules given above, the Codes of Practice give general guidance regarding the conduct of searches. These include: carrying out searches with courtesy, consideration and respect; minimising embarrassment;

conducting a search within reasonable time; and gaining the co-operation of the suspect wherever possible;

- where a suspect has not been arrested a record should be made by the police officer who conducted the search. If this is done on the spot a copy should then be given to the suspect immediately afterwards. Otherwise the record should be completed later and a copy may be applied for by the suspect within a year of the incident. Sometimes it is not possible for the police to complete a search record, such as where they are urgently called elsewhere;

- although the PACE Codes of Practice state that reasonable force may be used if a suspect refuses to co-operate in a search, this is not expressly stated under section 23(2) MDA 1971. However, if someone does not co-operate in a drugs search, he or she may be arrested for obstruction under section 23(4) of the 1971 Act. Also, force may not be used to effect an intimate search or an x-ray or ultrasound scan if the suspect refuses to consent to it.

PACE search powers

Another police power to search people exists under section 32 of PACE. This enables a police officer to search someone who has been arrested away from a police station and where they have reasonable grounds to believe that the suspect may be a danger to himself or herself or to other people. The police also have the power to search the arrested person for anything that could assist his or her escape, or which might be evidence of an offence. The extent of searches in public under section 32 is also restricted to the removal of an outer coat, jacket or gloves, but the provision also authorises the searching of a suspect's mouth. The search power under section 32 is relevant to drug enforcement because controlled substances have often been found on suspects who were arrested for other offences.

Civilian searches

In recent years, designated civilians such as escort officers and detention officers, have been given limited police powers in a range of circumstances. Escort officers have powers to transport arrested persons to police stations and may take them elsewhere for investigative purposes. They may also search arrested suspects as well as seize and retain anything found during this procedure. Detention officers have been given police powers enabling them to perform a number of routine duties in the custody suites at police stations. These include the taking of samples, as well as searching, photographing and fingerprinting suspects.

The civilianisation of certain police duties has more recently been extended to civilian 'staff custody officers'. These are gradually replacing police officers performing the role of custody officer, and are responsible for supervising the functions of custody suites at police stations.

The most visible use of designated civilians in the exercise of certain police powers can be seen in the role of the community support officer (CSO). The powers of CSOs include searching people whom they are empowered to detain for the purpose of seizing items that may cause injury or assist escape. They may also search for, and seize, alcohol and tobacco from young persons. If a CSO discovers a controlled drug that is believed to be unlawfully in someone's possession, whether or not it is found during any of the searches that a CSO may undertake, the CSO may seize and retain that drug. It is important to note that this does not give CSOs a specific power to stop and search persons for drugs.

POLICE SEARCHES OF PREMISES FOR DRUGS

Many drug offences occur away from the streets and other public places. For this reason the police need to rely on their powers to enter and search premises in order to obtain evidence of drug crimes as well as to prevent further offences in connection with controlled substances. Police powers to enter and search premises are available with or without search warrants.

Search *without* a warrant
Section 32 of PACE was mentioned above regarding police powers to search people on arrest. There is another aspect of section 32 that enables the police to enter premises without warrant on the arrest of a suspect provided that it is in connection with an indictable offence (in broad terms a serious offence: the definition of this term is given towards the end of this chapter).

Before the arrested person is taken to a police station, the police may enter and search any premises the suspect was in at the time of the arrest or was in immediately beforehand. This power may be used whether or not the arrested person occupied or controlled the premises. For instance, it may be a house owned or occupied by someone else where the suspect has concealed a quantity of drugs and when he or she was arrested in or near those premises.

Section 18 of PACE provides the police with another power to enter and search premises without warrant. In such cases the suspect may have been arrested several miles from his or her premises, but the police have the power to enter and search premises occupied or owned by the arrested person such as the suspect's home. Ultimately, the authority to do this should be given by a police officer of at least the rank of inspector; and this power may only be used when the suspect has been arrested for an indictable offence (below). Also, section 17 of PACE, among other things, enables the police to enter and search premises without warrant in order to arrest a person for an indictable offence (below).

Although a suspect may not initially have been arrested for a drugs related offence, it is quite common for evidence of such offences (and others) to be discovered when the police exercise their powers under sections 17, 18 and 32. For instance, people arrested for burglary often commit this crime in order to fund their drug habit and drugs may be found when their homes, or other premises, are searched.

Another power to enter and search premises without warrant can be found under section 23(1) MDA 1971. This empowers the police (or other authorised persons) to enter the premises of someone who is carrying on business as a producer or supplier of any controlled drugs. They may then demand the production of any documents relating to that business and inspect them accordingly - as well as any stocks of drugs held in those premises.

Search *with* a warrant
Section 23(3) MDA 1971 enables the police to apply for a search warrant from a magistrate where 'there is reasonable ground for suspecting' that someone is in unlawful possession of controlled drugs in any premises, or there are documents in those premises relating to drug dealing. Another entry and search power available to the police exists under section 8 of PACE. This enables the police to obtain a search warrant on the basis of reasonable grounds for believing that an indictable offence (below) has been committed and that there is evidence on specified premises relating to that offence. As the vast majority of drug offences

are classed as indictable, a section 8 warrant may be appropriate in many cases.

Warrants obtained under section 8 must be executed within three months and they may authorise entry on more than one occasion or even unlimited entries may be authorised; although these must be justified when making the application. The warrant need not be limited to a single set of premises. Where necessary, entry into more than one premises can be authorised under a 'specific premises' warrant. Where premises are owned or controlled by someone named in the application, but any of those premises cannot be identified, an 'all premises' warrant may be authorised. Reasonable force may be used, if necessary, in the execution of a warrant of entry and search.

In addition to the designated civilians mentioned earlier, civilian 'investigating officers' have been given certain police powers to conduct criminal investigations. Among other things, they may apply for warrants under section 8 of PACE and execute these accordingly; and that includes powers to seize and retain evidence found on premises. Civilian investigating officers have also been given the power to enter and search premises without warrant under section 18 of PACE.

POLICE POWERS OF ARREST

Arrest *with* a warrant

Only a minority of arrests are made under the authority of a warrant. The most frequently used warrants are those obtained under the Magistrates' Courts Act 1980. These apply to adults suspected of having committed an imprisonable offence and whose whereabouts are unknown for the service of a summons; or where someone has failed to attend court in answer to a summons provided that the offence is serious enough. As almost every drug offence is potentially punishable by imprisonment, a warrant for a drug suspect's arrest can usually be obtained under the latter criteria where an arrest warrant in the first instance is appropriate.

Arrest *without* a warrant

As far as drug offences are concerned, and indeed all crimes, the main focus of police powers of arrest without warrant is now focused on section 24 of PACE. The original version of section 24 stated different criteria empowering the police to make arrests. This was based on whether an offence was classed as 'arrestable'. To a large extent, this was based on the seriousness of the offence or its connection with more serious offences. This has now been superseded by the criteria of necessity, based around the nature and circumstances of the offence. This means that those holding the office of constable may arrest someone for *any* offence provided that certain conditions exist that make it necessary. The new version of section 24 of PACE provides that a constable may arrest without a warrant:

- anyone who is about to commit an offence;
- anyone who is in the act of committing an offence;
- anyone whom he has reasonable grounds for suspecting to be about to commit an offence;
- anyone whom he has reasonable grounds for suspecting to be committing an offence;
- if a constable has reasonable grounds for suspecting that an offence has been committed, he may arrest without a warrant anyone whom he has reasonable grounds to suspect of being guilty of it; and
- if an offence has been committed, a constable may arrest without a warrant -
  - anyone who is guilty of the offence; or
  - anyone whom he has reasonable grounds for suspecting to be guilty of it.

Section 24 goes on to provide that the powers of arrest stated above are exercisable only if the constable has reasonable grounds for believing that it is necessary to make an arrest where the following conditions exist:

- where the suspect's name and/or address cannot be ascertained;
- to prevent the suspect from doing the following— causing physical injury to his or herself or any other person; suffering physical injury; causing loss of or damage to property; committing an offence against public decency; or causing an unlawful obstruction of the highway;
- to protect a child or other vulnerable person from the suspect;

- to allow the prompt and effective investigation of the offence or of the conduct of the suspect; or
- to prevent any prosecution for the offence from being hindered by the disappearance of the suspect.

These new and potentially wide-ranging powers were introduced by the Serious Organised Crime and Police Act 2005. At the time they came into force a new Code of Practice governing police arrests also came into effect. This is the first time that a such a code has applied to police arrest powers and is designed to ensure that the police do not have completely unfettered powers of arrest; in other words they must comply with the provisions of the code and can be held accountable as to how they exercise these powers.

Citizen's arrest

The basis of non-police officers making arrests was also formerly based on whether the offence was arrestable. This has also changed under a new section 24A of PACE that relates to indictable offences (below) instead of the now defunct 'arrestable offence'. Section 24A states that a person other than a constable may arrest without a warrant—

- anyone who is in the act of committing an indictable offence;
- anyone whom he has reasonable grounds for suspecting to be committing an indictable offence;
- where an indictable offence has been committed, a person other than a constable may arrest without a warrant— anyone who is guilty of the offence; or anyone whom he has reasonable grounds for suspecting to be guilty of it.

Note that under section 24A, non-police officers do not have the power to arrest in order to prevent an indictable offence from being committed. Although the power to do this is absent under PACE, section 3 of the Criminal Law Act 1967 enables any person to use reasonable force in order to prevent crime. However, this must be exercised in a reasonable and proportionate manner.

The powers under section 24A of PACE are exercisable only if it appears to the person making the arrest that it is not reasonably practicable for a police officer to make it instead; and the person making the arrest has reasonable grounds for believing that an arrest is necessary to prevent the suspect causing physical injury to himself or herself or any other person, suffering physical injury, causing loss of or damage to property, or making off before the police arrive.

In practice, non-police officers are advised to exercise great caution when considering making an arrest. This is best left in the hands of the police unless there are very exceptional circumstances. Not only are there physical dangers and risks attached to making arrests but there are also potential legal dangers. In the increasingly litigious culture in this country, there are many who would not hesitate to sue a public-spirited citizen who acted in good faith but who made a mistake. The police are largely protected from personal civil liability as are certain civilian security professionals. It is therefore important to note the significant and continuing differences between the police and ordinary citizens' powers of arrest as described above.

WHAT IS AN INDICTABLE OFFENCE?

As mentioned earlier in this chapter, the vast majority of drug offences are classed as indictable. Primarily this legal term refers to offences that are triable only on indictment but it also, curiously, extends to offences that are triable either way. Offences that are triable only on indictment can only be tried before a jury in the Crown Court because they are among the most serious of all crimes. They include murder, manslaughter, rape, robbery and such like. There is no choice but for the person accused of such crimes to be tried and, if convicted, sentenced before the Crown Court. In the case of triable either way offences, these may be tried either before a magistrates' court or the Crown Court. The venue of any trial in either way cases depends upon a procedure known as mode of trial (or determining venue) whereby the magistrates' court decides, after listening to any representations by the accused or his or her advocate, whether the case is more suitable for summary trial or trial in the Crown Court.[1] Generally, the more serious drug offenders are brought before the Crown Court to be tried and sentenced in view of the greater sentencing powers available to judges in that court compared to those in the magistrates' court. [2]

---

[1] Various refinements to this procedure are beyond the scope of this work.

[2] Magistrates can normally sentence to up to six months per either way offence or 12 months in aggregate, i.e. re several offences. Beyond this they can commit to the Crown Court for sentence in certain instances. At the time of writing, an increase to 12 moths per offence and 15 months in aggregate, together with abolition of the power of

Examples of some of the more well-known triable either way offences are: theft, affray, assault occasioning actual bodily harm (ABH), burglary, simple criminal damage (under £5000), obtaining property by deception, as well as the majority of offences under the MDA 1971.

The indictable offence proviso also enables the police to enter and search premises without a warrant under section 18 of PACE, as mentioned above. The criteria of an offence being indictable also applies to several other police powers that may be used to combat drug-related crime. For instance, road blocks may be authorised under section 4 of PACE if the matter in question involves an indictable offence, or a suspect may be kept in police detention without charge, beyond the normal 36 hour maximum period, if the alleged offence is indictable and magistrates' court authorises this. It can therefore be seen that although the police may make an arrest without warrant for *any* offence, if it is serious enough to be classed as indictable, then other police powers can be invoked.

POLICE POWERS TO TEST FOR DRUGS

Sections 63B and 63C of PACE enable the police to require arrested people to provide a urine or a non-intimate sample in order to ascertain if certain drugs are present in their body. The reason for this power is to assist in making bail decisions, and also to make a sentencing decision if the suspect is convicted, as well as to facilitate any advice and treatment that may be open or available to that person. The main elements of these provisions are as follows:

- the arrested person must be aged at least 14 years;
- he or she must have been charged with a 'trigger offence' (below).
- the purpose of the test is to see whether 'specified' Class A drugs (below) are in the suspect's body.
- if the arrested person has been charged with any other crime that is not a 'trigger' offence, a police inspector or someone above that rank may authorise a test for specified Class A drugs. This must be based on the officer having reasonable

---

committal for sentence, as contained in the Criminal Justice Act 2003 has been placed on hold together with various other fundamental changes to magistrates' powers with regard to 'sentences below 12 months'. See, generally, *Criminal Justice Act 2003: A Guide to the New Procedures and Sentencing* (2004), Gibson B, Waterside Press.

grounds for suspecting that the arrested person's misuse of specified Class A drugs contributed to the offence charged.
- if the arrested person is under the age of 17 years, an appropriate adult (namely a parent, guardian, or social worker etc.) must be present during the complete procedure.

Trigger offences are theft, robbery, burglary, aggravated burglary, vehicle theft, aggravated vehicle taking, obtaining property by deception, going equipped for stealing, and unlawfully possessing, producing, supplying, or possessing with intent to supply heroin, cocaine, or 'crack' cocaine. 'Specified' Class A drugs are heroin, cocaine and 'crack' cocaine (but this list can be amended at some future date).

Extended Police Drug Testing Power

The original scheme has been extended by a further power that runs alongside it. This involves people aged 18 and above who have been arrested for a trigger offence, or any offence where a police inspector or someone above that rank reasonably believes that the misuse of a specified Class A drug caused or contributed to it. This will apply after the arrest of the suspect even if that person is not later charged. Any arrested suspect who fails, without good cause, to provide a sample commits an offence and should be warned about this beforehand.

OTHER ROLES FOR THE POLICE

The roles of the police are not solely confined to law-enforcement. Apart from taking part in drug awareness education in schools and other places, they also operate drug arrest referral schemes in police stations. Since 2000, this applies to all police forces. Such schemes provide various levels of assistance ranging from giving arrested people leaflets or other documents containing details of drug agencies, to giving them direct access to drug workers in police stations.

On 1 April 2006, the Serious Organized Crime Agency (SOCA) became operational. This new law-enforcement body has a wide remit which includes combating drug trafficking. In order to deal with all aspects of organized crime, officers from SOCA may be given police powers for specific purposes. Many of the powers and procedures outlined in this chapter may therefore be exercised by officers from SOCA as well as those within the police service; whilst, as already noted, SOCA can use other powers not dependent on prosecution, conviction, or even the presence in the UK of a suspect or target of their activities.

CHAPTER 9

Further Drug Testing Powers

As part of modern-day changes in law, procedure and practice, the drug testing of people charged with criminal offences extends to several other parts of the criminal justice system.

THE GENERIC COMMUNITY SENTENCE

This sentencing option has been available since April 2005, and contains a menu of requirements that may be attached to it. As far as convicted drug offenders aged at least 16 years are concerned, the most important is a drug rehabilitation requirement. This may be imposed if the court is satisfied that the offender is dependant on any controlled drug, or has a propensity to misuse it. It must also be established that the offender's drug problem is treatable and that he or she has consented to treatment. A treatment and testing period may then be imposed under the community sentence lasting at least six months. During this time the offender will receive drug rehabilitation treatment, including drug testing, as either a full-time resident at a specified institution or a non-resident. In any event, the offender will be under the supervision of a responsible officer who will monitor his or her progress, including by taking part in monthly reviews of the drug rehabilitation requirement.

The other requirements that may be attached to a community sentence are as follows, one or more of which may also be attached in addition to a drug rehabilitation requirement, depending on the offender's circumstances and the nature of the offence:

- an unpaid work requirement;
- an activity requirement;
- a programme requirement;
- a prohibited activity requirement;
- a curfew requirement;
- an exclusion requirement;
- a residence requirement;
- a mental health treatment requirement;

- an alcohol treatment requirement;
- a supervision requirement; and
- an attendance centre requirement.

It should also be noted that electronic monitoring may be attached to any community order in order to ensure compliance with it.[1]

OTHER DRUG TESTING POWERS

Drug treatment and testing has been extended to several other aspects of the criminal justice process, in summary:

- if a defendant aged 18 years or above, misuses specified Class A drugs (heroin, cocaine or 'crack' cocaine), that person will be required to undergo assessment and treatment for their drug misuse as a condition of bail. Bail may be denied by the court if the defendant refuses.

- offenders aged 14 years or above may be tested for any specified Class A drugs where a court is considering passing a community sentence or a suspended sentence. If the offender is under 17 years old an appropriate adult must be present. Failure to provide a sample without reasonable excuse is punishable by a fine not exceeding £2,500 in the case of an adult (or less in the case of a juvenile).

- a drug rehabilitation requirement lasting no less than six months may be imposed by a court as part of a suspended sentence order, i.e. when a sentence of imprisonment is imposed but suspend for up to two years. This requirement will include drug treatment and testing and can apply to an offender who misuses any controlled drug who can be treated, and who gives his or her consent. Failure to comply with a drug rehabilitation requirement (after a warning has been given but unheeded), will lead to any of the following consequences: the court invoking the original term and custodial period that was initially suspended or; substitution

---

[1] For a fuller explanation of the generic order itself and when it can be used, see *Criminal Justice Act 2003: A Guide to the New Procedures and Sentencing* (2004), Gibson B, Waterside Press.

of a lesser term and/or substitution of a lesser custodial period. Alternatively, the court may impose more demanding community requirements, or extend the supervision period, or extend the operational (suspension) period.

- prisoners and other people in custody aged at least 14 years who are released on parole or its equivalent, must provide a body sample if they misuse any specified Class A drug and this misuse played a part in their previous offending, or where this may cause them to re-offend. If the offender is under 17 years old an appropriate adult must be present.

- young offenders given an action plan order or a supervision order (i.e. normally by a youth court), may also have a drug treatment and testing requirement attached to any of those orders. This will apply if that person is addicted to, or otherwise misuses any drugs, and can be treated. Consent to this inclusion must be given if the person is aged over 14 years.

- prisoners may be required to provide a urine sample or any non-intimate sample, for drug testing by prison officers or prisoner custody officers. A positive drug test or a refusal to provide a sample for drug testing, constitute offences against Prison Rules and could result in disciplinary action being taken against the prisoner. Mandatory drug testing is intended to reduce the supply and demand for drugs in prisons and subsequently prevent physical or psychological harm to prisoners, including the reduction of drug-related intimidation. It also helps to identify prisoners who have drug problems so that help can be offered to them accordingly.

CHAPTER 10

Future Developments

Although the focus of this book has been on the legal aspects of drug misuse, it is important to conclude this coverage with other issues that affect this area of increasing concern. A useful insight into some of the social and political dimensions associated with the misuse of drugs, can be seen in various parts of the Fifth Report of the House of Commons Select Committee on Science and Technology (the 'Committee'), together with the official responses. The title of this report is *Drug Classification – Making a Hash of It?* and this constituted a major inquiry that addressed, among many other things, the classification of illicit drugs within the context of scientific advice and evidence. In the course of its investigations, the Committee placed the Advisory Council on the Misuse of Drugs (the 'ACMD') under close scrutiny, particularly in terms of its composition and the way its business is conducted. Approximately three months after the Committee had published its report, both the Government and ACMD officially responded to the 50 wide-ranging findings contained within it.

The Government's responses were expressed through the medium of a Command Paper (Cm 6941) that was laid before Parliament on 13 October 2006. On the same date, the chair of the ACMD sent his responses to the chairman of the Committee in the form of a report and covering letter.

GOVERNMENT AND ACMD RESPONSES

Whilst acknowledging the ACMD's importance in terms of its remit under the Misuse of Drugs Act 1971 (see *Chapter 2*), the Committee considered that there were a number of serious flaws in its overall workings. These included a lack of clarity regarding its remit, with particular reference to the consideration of social harm attached to illicit drugs. On this issue, the Committee also identified what it considered to be a perturbing divergence of views between the chair of the ACMD and the then Home Secretary. Both the Government and ACMD denied certain aspects of these conclusions and cited several reports produced by the ACMD in which 'social harm' was clearly addressed. They also denied that contradictory views were expressed by the chair of the

ACMD and the (previous) Home Secretary, although the reasons for their opinions do not seem to be very clear.

Other structural and procedural items concerning the ACMD

Further unease was expressed by the Committee regarding the apparent lack of clarity in the role of the Association of Chief Police Officers (ACPO), which is represented on the ACMD. The ACMD and the Government countered this assertion by praising the work of the ACPO representatives and emphasised the vitally important role of police intelligence in the ACMD's decisions.

Criticism was also made regarding the disproportionately large amount of time and resources that the ACMD devoted to advising the Home Office instead of interacting with other government departments. The Government and the ACMD responded by stating that representatives from the Scottish Executive, the Welsh Assembly and the Northern Ireland Assembly, were invited to attend most ACMD meetings, as well as representatives from the Department for Education and Skills and the Department of Health. In the case of these two government departments, the ACMD stated that it had interacted with them on several important issues and wondered why the Committee considered its links with other departments to be lacking. Concerns were raised regarding the ACMD's lack of transparency in certain aspects of its work, although it was praised by the Committee for its openness and clarity when describing its decision-making process when classifying drugs. The Committee suggested that the agendas and minutes of ACMD meetings should be routinely published and went so far as to suggest the holding of open meetings that could be attended by the public.

In both cases the chair of the ACMD argued in response that occasionally sensitive information obtained from law-enforcement agencies arose during meetings which should not be made public. However, the Committee stated that such information could be removed from the minutes where necessary and the public could be excluded when such matters were raised. The Government, however, responded by supporting greater transparency of the ACMD's work and the ACMD subsequently stated its commitment to achieving this objective, whilst exercising due caution regarding sensitive material.

Despite endorsing the ACMD's practice of using experts in sub-committees and working groups, the Committee would not comment on whether its membership was appropriately balanced but stated that it would become unwieldy and unmanageable if it became even larger. There were already 37 members of the ACMD at the time the report was published and the Committee stated that it would oppose any further increase. It also expressed concern regarding the selection of ACMD members when it seemed to them that the chair played a major part in advising the Home Secretary as to who should be appointed. Although it was natural to use the chair's expertise during this process, the Committee felt that he could potentially exert a very powerful influence on the composition of the ACMD. However, it acknowledged that due process had been followed during the appointment of members because of the presence of an independent assessor, although such a person needed to have the relevant scientific and technical expertise to judge who should be appointed. It therefore recommended that in future the Chief Scientific Adviser to the Home Office should oversee the selection of ACMD members. The official response was that the membership of the ACMD was very wide and included police officers, judges, magistrates, voluntary organizations and teachers. It therefore went beyond the scope of a conventional scientific advisory body and in consequence the Home Office Chief Scientific Adviser will not play a part in selecting individual members of the ACMD; however, where appropriate, he or she will give advice regarding its overall composition.

Further attention was directed towards the chair of the ACMD regarding his or her period of office which the Committee recommended should be for a maximum of five years instead of the current ten years. Although the present holder was effective and respected, the Committee were concerned as to whether such a post should be occupied by *anyone* for as much as ten years. It then added that the same person could be re-appointed as an ordinary member and still serve up to the ten year maximum. Both the Government and ACMD rejected this proposition on the grounds that the maximum period in office of chairs of other Non-Departmental Public Bodies is limited to ten years. All members, including the chair, are subject to satisfactory appraisals, and the Home Secretary is empowered to refuse the re-appointment of the chair or to dismiss him or her at any time. Concern was expressed when it was discovered that the ACMD does not have its own staff nor its own budget. Instead, a secretariat was provided by Home Office staff and this brought into question whether this could affect the ACMD's independence. The Committee stated that the ACMD must be subject to independent oversight and recommended that the Home Office should commission independent reviews of it at least every five years. The ACMD defended its secretariat, stating that it adopted an impartial and supportive role, and the Government stated that an independent review of the ACMD had already been announced in July 2006.

During the inquiry, it was noted that certain classes of people were not represented on the ACMD. No-one with past experience of misusing drugs or receiving mental health treatment was included, neither was there a representative from any charity that focuses on prevention before harm reduction. Schedule 1 to the MDA 1971 states that the ACMD must consist of at least 20 members and there shall be at least one person on the ACMD who has wide and recent experience representing each of the following activities:

- the practice of medicine (other than veterinary medicine);
- the practice of dentistry;
- the practice of veterinary medicine;
- the practice of pharmacy;
- the pharmaceutical industry;
- chemistry other than pharmaceutical chemistry.

Schedule 1 also stipulates that people with wide and recent experience of social problems connected with the misuse of drugs, shall also be included on the ACMD. The Government agreed with the Committee when it emphasised the importance of having a diversity of expertise within the membership of the ACMD, and in turn this body stated that its responsibilities are fulfilled through the wide range of expertise represented on it.

Cannabis and magic mushrooms

In order to ascertain the processes used in making drug classification decisions, including the role of scientific advice and evidence, the Committee looked at the classification of cannabis, magic mushrooms and amphetamines (including ecstasy and methylamphetamine). Their report cited the confusion that was caused (which still continues to a significant extent), when cannabis was reclassified in 2004. The Committee strongly criticised the inadequate publicity that accompanied this exercise and warned that any further changes in policy regarding this drug should not be allowed to cause further confusion. The Government refused to fully admit that it caused confusion as a result of inadequate communication but accepted that, if there are any further changes in policy, then it had a responsibility to make sure that this was communicated in a clear and coherent manner. Before departing from the issues regarding cannabis, the Committee considered the controversial *Gateway Theory* which subscribes to the view that the use of this drug constitutes a pathway to the misuse of harder drugs. The Committee stated unequivocally that this theory was not supported by any conclusive evidence to which the Government agreed accordingly.

The Committee then reported its findings in respect of magic mushrooms which, on 18 July 2005, were classified as Class A drugs. Previously, only the drug obtained from these fungi, namely psilocin, was a controlled substance. This created an anomaly in the law, exacerbated by substantial imports of these mushrooms that were being sold openly from market stalls and in shops. The Government therefore decided to bring the fungus itself under the control of the MDA 1971. Although psilocin and its esters such as psilocybin are hallucinogenic substances, many have disputed their inclusion under Class A. Even the chair of the ACMD admitted that he could not explain the rationale behind the inclusion of this drug under Class A in 1970 and 1971. The Home Office also admitted that it could not explain the reason for this, having never conducted any research into this drug or found evidence of any link between use of this drug and acquisitive crime, or to offending more generally.

A lack of research evidence and consultation
This was not the first occasion during the inquiry where a lack of research on drugs seemed apparent. Elsewhere in their report, the Committee remarked that there was a lack of investment in addiction research in this country compared to other developed nations, and criticised the ACMD for failing to exert sufficient pressure on the Government to rectify this. The ACMD repudiated this criticism by citing several if its recent publications where recommendations were made for further research. The Government added its own voice by stating that the Home Office as well as other bodies such as the Department of Health, the Scottish Executive and the Medical Research Council, have all undertaken significant research, although it conceded that this could be co-ordinated more effectively.

According to the Committee's report, when the Government decided to place magic mushrooms under Class A (see under previous heading), this was not a classification decision but a clarification of the law. This meant that the Government did not have to consult with the ACMD in accordance with the usual practice. Although the Government wrote to the ACMD requesting an opinion, it was stated that the evidence was not fully reviewed. The Committee therefore accused the Government of contravening the spirit of the MDA 1971 as this deprived the ACMD of the opportunity to properly consider the evidence. The Government's response contained a firm rejection of this criticism. It explained the necessity for drug laws to be clear and unambiguous and then pointed to the grey area in the law where the legal status of the magic mushroom (above) was uncertain. The Government further stated that it took the opportunity to clarify the law expeditiously by using the Drugs Act 2005 as the medium for this purpose.

It was also asserted that the ACMD was given the opportunity to give advice even though there was no requirement to do so under the

MDA 1971. However, the Committee went further and accused the chair of the ACMD of complacency regarding the placement of magic mushrooms under Class A, and rebuked the ACMD for failing to oppose the intentions of the Government. The ACMD strongly repudiated this assertion and stated that the Committee was lacking in knowledge of the basic principles of pharmacology. It went on to explain the main characteristics of the hallucinogenic drugs psilocin and psilocybin that are contained within the magic mushroom, adding that the pharmacological effect of consuming fresh mushrooms is no less than that attributable to the dried forms of this fungi. The ACMD further added that it was plain common sense that there should be no difference in the classification of fresh or dried mushrooms and it therefore supported the Government's proposals.[1]

Ecstasy and 'crystal meth'

The Committee's report went on to provide a brief description of the general characteristics of ecstasy and amphetamine. It then concentrated in more detail on the drug ecstasy, expressing disappointment that such a well-known and widely used drug has never had its Class A status reviewed by the ACMD; an urgent review of ecstasy's classification was therefore recommended. But the Government's reaction was very clear on this issue – it stated, quite simply, that it has no intention of reclassifying Ecstasy and that it will remain a Class A drug. The ACMD, however, appeared to be more open-minded and stated that it will examine the available evidence and if this is strong enough it will review the status of this substance.

The Committee's inquiries into the drug methylamphetamine (commonly known as 'crystal meth' or 'ice'), disclosed a number of disturbing features. First, it is now the world's most widely manufactured illicit synthetic drug. Secondly, the ACMD appeared to have made a U-turn, having initially advised the Government not to reclassify this drug from Class B to Class A but having changed its mind about six months later. According to the Committee's findings, the ACMD was originally reluctant to recommend upgrading methylamphetamine because there did not appear to be evidence of its widespread misuse in this country. But a more important reason for this decision was based on the ACMD's concerns that drug users might be more attracted to the drug if it were made Class A. This caused the

---

[1] It should be noted that the process by which the Government made magic mushrooms a Class A drug was via Section 21 of the Drugs Act 2005. The use of primary legislation rather than delegated legislation to achieve this purpose was a deviation from the normal procedure when classifying controlled drugs (see *Chapter 2*).

Committee to express serious concern and in turn accused the ACMD of making a political judgement on this issue. The Committee added that the ACMD's sudden change in direction conveyed the impression that it either reacted to external pressure or had realised that it had made a mistake. The report went on to state that the ACMD changed its mind because of a rise in the use of methylamphetamine and the emergence of illicit laboratories producing this drug, as well as greater media interest in this substance. Also, it was realised that if this drug were to be reclassified as a Class A drug, this would mean that 'ice houses' would be subject to the same police closure powers as 'crack houses' (see *Chapter 6*). The Committee welcomed the subsequent recommendation to upgrade methylamphetamine to Class A but pointed out that all of this information had been predicted by a number of other commentators.

The Government robustly defended the ACMD against the accusation that it had made a political judgement and stated that it had not acted improperly by taking into account the social risks associated with this drug. It added that the ACMD is different from conventional scientific advisory bodies and that it had acted within its remit. In a similar fashion, the ACMD rejected the suggestion that it had changed its mind regarding the reclassification of methylamphetamine because it had realised that it had made a mistake, or had succumbed to outside pressure. Although it decided not to recommend upgrading this drug in November 2005, it did so on the understanding that it would review the situation a year later. If the position changed in the meantime, it was agreed that an urgent meeting would be convened. As this chapter is being written the reclassification process has already started and this drug should be included under Class A by late-2006 or the early part of 2007. Already, a draft statutory instrument has been laid before Parliament for its scrutiny prior to being presented to The Queen for enactment before the Privy Council (see *Chapter 2*).

The classification system for drugs

Much of the Committee's attention was directed towards the current system of classifying controlled drugs into A, B or C, and its effectiveness. It reported that many anomalies had been discovered in the course of the inquiry and it was stated that the existing system is 'not fit for purpose'. Strong criticism was made of the ACMD for its failure to bring this to the attention of the Home Secretary at an earlier stage.

The Committee strongly urged that the entire system of classifying drugs should be reviewed with particular reference to developing a scale of harm that is more scientifically based. However, the Government announced in its reply that it has abandoned the suggested review of the current drug classification system. It believes that it has stood the test of time, and that it fully and effectively discharges its function. The report goes on to state that a clear and meaningful distinction is made between the controlled drugs due to the existing A,B,C classification system. The Government believes that it is widely understood that Class A drugs attract the highest criminal sanctions because they are the most harmful whereas Class C drugs are not in the same category, although they are still harmful.

A more holistic approach?

But is a more holistic approach going to be taken regarding the entire issue of substance abuse in the future? The following extract from a report compiled by the ACMD,[2] indicates a possible move in this direction:

In its first 30 years, the ACMD has focused most of its attention on drugs that are subject to the controls and restrictions of the Misuse of Drugs Act [1971]. Although its terms of reference do not prevent it from doing so, the ACMD has not considered alcohol and tobacco other than tangentially. The scientific evidence is now clear that nicotine and alcohol have pharmacological actions similar to other psychoactive drugs. Both cause serious health and social problems and there is growing evidence of very strong links between the use of tobacco, alcohol and other drugs. For the ACMD to neglect two of the most harmful psychoactive drugs simply because they have a different legal status no longer seems appropriate.

---

[2] Advisory Council on the Misuse of Drugs (September 2006) *Pathways to Problems: Hazardous use of tobacco, alcohol and other drugs by young people in the UK and its implications for policy* (page 14). Reproduced under Crown Copyright.

Appendix 1: List of Controlled Drugs

Schedule 2 to the Misuse of Drugs Act 1971

(The Schedule under the Misuse of Drugs Regulations 2001 in which each drug is listed is shown in brackets: see *Chapters 1* and 3)

PART I CLASS A DRUGS

1(a)

Acetorphine (2)
Alfentanil (2)
Allylprodine (2)
Alphacetylmethadol (2)
Alphameprodine (2)
Alphamethadol (2)
Alphaprodine (2)
Anileridine (2)
Benzethidine (2)
Benzylmorphine (2)
Betacetylmethadol (2)
Betameprodine (2)
Betamethadol (2)
Betaprodine (2)
Bezitramide (2)
Bufotenine (1)
Carfentanil (2)
Clonitazene (2)
Coca leaf (1)
Cocaine (2)
Desomorphine (2)
Dextromoramide (2)
Diamorphine (2)
Diampromide (2)
Diethylthiambutene (2)
Difenoxin (2) (1-(3-cyano-3,3-
   diphenylpropyl)
   -4-phenylpiperidine-4-carboxylic
   acid)
Dihydrocodeinone
   O-carboxymethyloxime (2)
Dihydroetorphine (2)
Dihydromorphine (2)
Dimenoxadole (2)
Dimepheptanol (2)
Dimethylthiambutene (2)
Dioxaphetylbutyrate (2)
Diphenoxylate (2)
Dipipanone (2)
Drotebanol (2) (3,4-dimethoxy-17-
   methylmorphinan-
6B,14-diol)
Ecgonine, and any derivative
of ecgonine which is
convertible to ecgonine or
to cocaine (2)
Ethylmethylthiambutene (2)
Eticyclidine (1)
Etonitazene (2)
Etorphine (2)
Etoxeridine (2)
Etryptamine (1)
Fentanyl (2)
Furethidine (2)
Hydrocodone ((2)
Hydromorphinal (2)
Hydromorphone (2)
Hydroxypethidine (2)
Isomethadone (2)
Ketobemidone (2)
Levomethorphan (2)
Levomoramide (2)
Levophenacylmorphan (2)
Levorphanol (2)
Lofentanil (2)
Lysergamide (1)
Lysergide and other N-alkyl
   derivatives of lysergamide (1)
Mescaline (1)
Metazocine (2)
Methadone (2)
Methadyl acetate (2)

Methyldesorphine (2)
Methyldihydro-morphine (2)
(6-methyldihydro-morphine)
Metopon (2)
Morpheridine (2)
Morphine (2)
Morphine methobromide, morphine
N-oxide and other pentavalent
nitrogen morphine derivatives (2)
Myrophine (2)
Nicomorphine [3,6-dinicotinoyl-
morphine] (2)
Noracymethadol (2)
Norlevorphanol (2)
Normethadone (2)
Normorphine (2)
Norpipanone (2)
Opium, whether raw, prepared (1)
or medicinal (2)
Oxycodone (2)
Oxymorphone (2)
Pethidine (2)
Phenadoxone (2)
Phenampromide (2)
Phenazocine (2)

Phencyclidine (2)
Phenomorphan (2)
Phenoperidine (2)
Piminodine (2)
Piritramide (2)
Poppy-straw and concentrate of
poppy-straw (1)
Proheptazine (2)
Properidine (2) (1-methyl-4-phenyl-
piperidine-4-carboxylic acid
isopropyl ester)
Psilocin (1) and any fungus *
containing Psilocin or an ester of
Psilocin (1)
Racemethorphan (2)
Racemoramide (2)
Racemorphan (2)
Remifentanil (2)
Rolicyclidine (1)
Sufentanil (2)
Tenocyclidine (1)
Thebacon (2)
Thebaine (2)
Tilidate (2)
Trimeperidine (2)

4-Bromo-2,5-dimethoxy-a-methylphenethylamine (1)
4-Cyano-2-dimethylamino-4,4-diphenylbutane (2)
4-Cyano-1-methyl-4-phenylpiperidine (2)
4-Methyl-aminorex 16 (1)
N,N-Diethyltryptamine (1)
N,N-Dimethyltryptamine (1)
2,5-Dimethoxy-a,4-dimethylphenethylamine (1)
N-Hydroxy-tenamphetamine (1)
1-Methyl-4-phenylpiperidine-4-carboxylic acid (2)
2-Methyl-3-morpholino-1,1-diphenylpropane-carboxylic acid (2)
4-Phenylpiperidine-4-carboxylic acid ethyl ester (2)

[* This fungus refers to the 'magic mushroom']

The following 35 'ecstasy' type drugs were included under Schedule 1 to the
Misuse of Drugs Regulations 2001 and under Class A on 1 February 2002:

(1)   Allyl (a-methyl-3,4-methylenedioxyphenethyl)amine. **'MDAL'**
(2)   2-amino-1-(2,5-dimethoxy-4-methylphenyl) ethanol. **'BOHD'**
(3)   2-amino-1-(3,4-dimethoxyphenyl) ethanol. **'DME'**
(4)   Benzyl (a-methyl-3,4-methylenedioxyphenethyl) amine. **'MDBZ'**
(5)   4-Bromo-B,2,5-tromethoxyphenethylamine. **'BOB'**
(6)   N-(4-sec-butylthio-2,5-dimethoxyphenethyl) hydroxylamine. **HOT-17**

(7)   Cyclopropylmethyl (a-methyl-3,4 methylenedioxyphenethyl) amine. **'MDCPM'**

(8)   2-(4,7-dimethoxy-2,3-dihydro-1H-indan-5-yl)ethylamine. **'2C-G3'**

(9)   2-(4,7-dimethoxy-2,3-dihydro-1H-indan-5-yl)-1-methylethylamine. **G3'**

(10)   2-(2,5-dimethoxy-4-methylphenyl) cyclopropylamine. **'DMCPA'**

(11)   2-(1,4-dimethoxy-2-napthyl) ethylamine. **'2C-G-N'**

(12)   2-(1,4-dimethoxy-2-napthyl-1-methylethylamine. **'G-N'**

(13)   N-(2,5-dimethoxy-4-propylthiopenthyl) hydroxylamine. **'HOT-7'**

(14)   2-(1,4-dimethoxy-5,6,7,8-tetrahydro-2-napthyl) ethylamine. **'2C-G-4'**

(15)   2-(1,4-dimethoxy-5,6,7,8-tetrahydro-2-napthyl)-1-methylethylamine. **'G-4'**

(16)   a,a-dimethyl-3,4-methylenedioxyphenethylamine. **'MDPH'**

(17)   a,a-dimethyl-3,4-methylenedioxyphenethyl) (methyl) amine. **'MDMP'**

(18)   Dimethyl (a-methyl-3,4-methylenedioxyphenethyl) amine. **'MDDM'**

(19)   N-(4-ethylthio-2,5-dimethoxyphenethyl) hydroxylamine. **'HOT-2'**

(20)   4-iodo-2,5-dimethoxy-a-methylphenethyl (dimethyl) amine. **'IDNNA'**

(21)   2-(1,4-methano-5,8-dimethoxy-1,2,3,4-tetrahydro-6-napthyl) ethylamine. **'2C-G-5'**

(22)   2-(1,4-methano-5,8-dimethoxy-1,2,3,4-tetrahydro-6-napthyl)-1-methylethylamine. **'G-5'**

(23)   2-(5-methoxy-2,2-dimethyl-2,3-dihydrobenzo [b] furan-6-yl)-1-methylethylamine. **'F-22'**

(24)   2-methoxyethyl (a-methyl-3,4-methylenedioxyphenethyl) amine. **'MDMEOET'**

(25)   2-(5-methoxy-2-methyl-2,3-dihydrobenzo [b] furan-6-yl)-1-methylethylamine. **'F-2'**

(26)   B-methoxy-3,4-methylenedioxyphenethylamine. **'BOH'**

(27)   1-(3,4-methylenedioxybenzyl) butyl (ethyl) amine. **'ETHYL-K'**

(28)   1-(3,4-methylenedioxybenzyl) butyl (methyl) amine. **'METHYL-K'**

(29)   2-(a-methyl-3,4-methylenedioxyphenethylamino) ethanol. **'MDHOET'**

(30)   a-methyl-3,4-methylenedioxyphenethyl (prop-2-ynyl) amine. **'MDPL'**

(31)   N-methyl-N-(a-methyl-3,4-methylenedioxyphenethyl) hydroxylamine. **'FLEA'**

(32)   O-methyl-N-(a-methyl-3,4-methylenedioxyphenethyl) hydroxylamine. **'MDMEO'**

(33)   B,3,4,5-tetramethoxyphenethylamine. **'BOM'**

(34)   B,2,5-trimethoxy-4-methylphenethylamine. **'BOD'**

(35)   4-Methylthioamphetamine. **'4-MTA'**

(also known as a-Methyl-4-(methylthio) phenethylamine).

(b) any compound (not being a compound for the time being specified in sub-paragraph (a) above) structurally derived from tryptamine or from a ring-hydroxy tryptamine by substitution at the nitrogen atom of the sidechain with one or more alkyl substituents but no other substituent;

(c) any compound (not being methoxyphenamine or a compound for the time being specified in sub-paragraph (a) above) structurally derived from phenethylamine, an N-alkylphenethylamine, a-methylphenethylamine, an N-alkyl-a-methylphenethylamine, [*this covers 'ecstasy' MDMA*] a-ethylphenethylamine, or an N-alkyl-a-ethylphenethylamine by substitution in the ring to any extent with alkyl, alkoxy, alkylenedioxy or halide substituents, whether or not further substituted in the ring by one or more other univalent substitutents.

(d) any compound (not being a compound for the time being specified in sub-paragraph (a) above) structurally derived from fentanyl by modification in any of the following ways, that is to say,

(i) by replacement of the phenyl portion of the phenethyl group by any heteromonocycle whether or not further substituted in the heterocycle;

(ii) by substitution in the phenethyl group with alkyl, alkenyl, alkoxy, hydroxy, halogeno, haloalkyl, amino or nitro groups;

(iii) by substitution in the piperidine ring with alkyl or alkenyl groups;

(iv) by substitution in the aniline ring with alkyl, alkoxy, alkylene-dioxy, halogeno, or haloalkyl groups;

(v) by substitution at the 4-position of the piperidine ring with any alkoxycarbonyl or acyloxy group;

(vi) by replacement of the N-propionyl group by another acyl group;

(e) any compound (not being a compound for the time being specified in sub-paragraph (a) above) structurally derived from pethidine by modification in any of the following ways, that is to say,

(i) by replacement of the 1-methyl group by an acyl,alkyl whether or not unsaturated, benzyl or phenethyl group, whether or not further substituted;

(ii) by substitution in the piperidine ring with alkyl or alkenyl groups or with a propano bridge, whether or not further substituted;

(iii) by substitution in the 4-phenyl ring with alkyl, alkoxy, arloxy, halogen or haloalkyl groups.

(iv) By replacement of the 4-ethoxycarbonyl by any other alkoxycarbonyl or any alkoxyalkyl or acyloxy group;

(v) By formation of an N-oxide or of a quaternary base.

2. Any stereoisomeric form of a substance for the time being specified in paragraph 1 above not being dextromethorphan or dextrorphan.

3. Any ester or ether of a substance for the time being specified in paragraph 1 or 2 above (not being a substance for the time being specified in Part II of this Schedule).

4. Any salt of a substance for the time being specified in any of paragraphs 1 to 3 above.

5. Any preparation or other product containing a substance or product for the time being specified in any of paragraphs 1 to 4 above.

6. Any preparation designed for administration by injection which includes a substance or product for the time being specified in any of paragraphs 1 to 3 of Part II of this Schedule *[In other words, any Class B drug prepared for injection becomes a Class A substance].*

PART II. CLASS B DRUGS

1(a)

Acetyldihydrocodeine (2)

Amphetamine (2)

Codeine (2)

Dihydrocodeine (2)

Ethylmorphine (2) (3-ethylmorphine)

Glutethimide (2)

Lefetamine (2)

Mecloqualone (2)

Methaqualone (2)

Methcathinone (1)

Methylamphetamine (2)**

Methylphenidate (2)

Methylphenobarbitone (3)

Nicocodine (2)

Nicodicodine

(6-nicotinoyldihydrocodeine) (2)

Norcodeine (2)

Pentazocine (3)

Phenmetrazine (2)

Pholcodine (2)

Propiram (2)
Quinalbarbitone (2)
Zipeprol (2)

a-methylphenethylhydroxylamine
N-hydroxyamphetamine (2) *

[*This ecstasy-type drug was included on 1 February 2002 as well as the other 35 ecstasy-type drugs although they were placed under Class A. ** Methylamphetamine is due to be a Class A drug from January 2007]

(b) any 5,5 disubstituted barbituric acid.

2. Any stereoisomeric form of a substance for the time being specified in paragraph 1 of this part of this Schedule.
3. Any salt of a substance for the time being specified in any of paragraphs 1 or 2 of this Part of this Schedule.
4. Any preparation or other product containing a substance or product for the time being specified in any of paragraphs 1 to 3 of this Part of this Schedule, not being a preparation falling within paragraph 6 of Part I of this Schedule.

PART III. CLASS C DRUGS

1.(a)

(Note that all the Schedule 4 drugs listed in this sub-paragraph are included in Part 1 of that Schedule.)

Alprazolam (4)
Aminorex (4)
Benzphetamine (3)
Bromazepam (4)
Brotizolam (4)
Buprenorphine (3)
Camazepam (4)
Cannabinol (1)
Cannabinol derivatives (1)
Cannabis & cannabis resin (1)
Cathine (3)
Cathinone (1)
Chlordiazepoxide (4)
Chlorphentermine (3)
Clobazam (4)
Clonazepam (4)
Clorazepic acid (4)
Clotiazepam (4)
Cloxazolam (4)
Delorazepam (4)
Dextropropoxyphene (2)
Diazepam (4)
Diethylpropion (3)
Dronabinol (2) *
Estazolam (4)

Ethchlorvynol (3)
Ethinamate (3)
Ethyl loflazepate (4)
Fencamfamin (4)
Fenethylline (2)
Fenproporex (4)
Fludiazepam (4)
Flunitrazepam (3)
Flurazepam (4)
Gammahydroxybutyrate   [4-Hydroxy-n-butyric acid] (4)
Halazepam (4)
Haloxazolam (4)
Ketazolam (4)
Ketamine (4)
Loprazolam (4)
Lorazepam (4)
Lormetazepam (4)
Mazindol (3)
Medazepam (4)
Mefenorex (4)
Mephentermine (3)
Meprobamate (3)
Mesocarb (4)
Methyprylone (3)

Midazolam (4)

Nimetazepam (4)

Nitrazepam (4)

Nordazepam (4)

Oxazepam (4)

Oxazolam (4)

Pemoline (4)

Phendimetrazine (3)

Phentermine (3)

Pinazepam (4)

Pipradol (3)

Prazepam (4)

Pyrovalerone (4)

Temazepam (3)

Tetrazepam (4)

Triazolam (4)

Zolpidem (4)

N-Ethylamphetamine (4)

(* This drug is a derivative of cannabinol but has been included separately for clarification).

2. Any stereoisomeric form of a substance for the time being specified in paragraph 1 of this part of this Schedule (not being phenylpropanolamine)

3. Any salt of a substance for the time being specified in any of paragraphs 1 or 2 of this Part of this Schedule.

4. Any preparation or other product containing a substance for the time being specified in any of paragraphs 1 to 3 of this Part of this Schedule.

(b) (All the drugs listed in this sub-paragraph are included under Part 2 of Schedule 4.)

Atamestane (4)

Bolandiol (4)

Bolasterone (4)

Bolazine (4)

Boldenone (4)

Bolenol (4)

Bolmantalate (4)

Calusterone (4)

4-Chlormethandienone (4)

Clostebol (4)

Drostanolone (4)

Enestebol (4)

Epitiostanol (4)

Ethyloestrenol (4)

Fluoxymesterone (4)

Formebolone (4)

Furazabol (4)

Mebolazine (4)

Mepitiostane (4)

Mesabolone (4)

Mestanolone (4)

Mesterolone (4)

Methandienone (4)

Methandriol (4)

Methenolone (4)

Methyltestosterone (4)

Metribolone (4)

Mibolerone (4)

Nandrolone (4)

Norboletone (4)

Norclostebol (4)

Norethandrolone (4)

Ovandrotone (4)

Oxabolone (4)

Oxandrolone (4)

Oxymesterone (4)

Oxymetholone (4)

Prasterone (4)

Propetandrol (4)

Quinbolone (4)

Roxibolone (4)

Silandrone (4)

Stanolone (4)

Stanozolol (4)

Stenbolone (4)

Testosterone (4)

Thiomesterone (4)

Trenbolone (4)

4-Androstene-3,17-dione (4)

19-Nor-4-Androstene-3,17-dione (4)

5-Androstene-3,17-diol (4)

19-Nor-5-Androstene-3,17-dione(4)

(c) any compound (not being Trilostane or a compound for the time being specified in sub-paragraph (b) above structurally derived from 17-hydroxyandrostan-3-one or from 17-hydroxyestran-3-one by modification in any of the following ways, that is to say,

(i) by further substitution at position 17 by a methyl or ethyl group;

(ii) by substitution to any extent at one or more of positions 1,2,4,6,7,9,11 or 16, but at no other position;

(iii) by unsaturation in the carbocyclic ring system to any extent, provided that there are no more than two ethylenic bonds in any carbocyclic ring;

(iv) by fusion of ring A with a heterocyclic system;

(d) any substance which is an ester or ether (or, where more than one hydroxyl function is available, both an ester and an ether) of a substance specified in sub-paragraph (b) or described in sub-paragraph (c) above; or of cannabinol or a cannabinol derivative. *[The last sentence was added when cannabis etc. was reclassified under Class C].*

(e) Chorionic Gonadotrophin (HCG) (4)
Clenbuterol (4)
Non-human chorionic gonadotrophin (4)
Somatotropin (4)
Somatrem (4)
Somatropin (4)

Appendix 2: The Development of Drugs Legislation

PHARMACY ACT 1868

Introduced national controls on the sale of 15 substances regarded as poisons. These included cocaine, opium, and opium based products.

POISONS & PHARMACY ACT 1908

Effected further controls over the sale of cocaine, opium and also morphine.

DEFENCE OF THE REALM REGULATIONS [40B] 1916 (MADE UNDER THE DEFENCE OF THE REALM ACT 1914)

Introduced restrictions on the unlawful possession of opium and cocaine.

DANGEROUS DRUGS ACTS 1920, 1925, 1932, 1951, 1964, 1965 & 1967

Regulated the import/export, manufacture, sale and possession of cocaine, heroin, morphine and opium; extended controls to cannabis and coca leaves; effected controls over LSD; introduced police powers to stop/search drug suspects.

DRUGS (PREVENTION OF MISUSE) ACT 1964

Introduced controls over amphetamine and pemoline.

MEDICINES ACT 1968

Governs the manufacture, supply and sale of medicinal products, including those which are controlled drugs.

MISUSE OF DRUGS ACT 1971

Consolidated all the existing law, and used the term 'controlled drugs' rather than dangerous drugs. Introduced a number of new drugs offences including possession with intent to supply, as well as extending the range of controlled drugs and making provision for future changes, and increasing the penalties for drugs offences.

CUSTOMS AND EXCISE MANAGEMENT ACT 1979

Prohibited, among other things, the unlawful import/export of controlled drugs.

CONTROLLED DRUGS (PENALTIES) ACT 1985

Increased the maximum prison sentences for trafficking in Class A drugs.

DRUG TRAFFICKING OFFENCES ACT 1986

Introduced confiscation orders and some additional money laundering offences, as well as new laws governing drug paraphernalia.

CRIMINAL JUSTICE (INTERNATIONAL CO-OPERATION) ACT 1990

Strengthened the Drug Trafficking Offences Act, regulated substances used to unlawfully produce controlled drugs, and created the offence of carrying/concealing controlled drugs on ships.

CRIMINAL JUSTICE ACT 1991

Created a statutory framework which enabled the courts to include drug/alcohol treatment within probation orders.

DRUG TRAFFICKING ACT 1994

Consolidated the existing law on drug trafficking

CRIMINAL JUSTICE AND PUBLIC ORDER ACT 1994

Introduced random drug testing in prisons, and increased the maximum fines in respect of certain Class B and C drug offences.

CRIME (SENTENCES) ACT 1997

Introduced a minimum sentence of 7 years imprisonment for 18 year olds and above convicted of a third Class A drug trafficking offence.

CRIME AND DISORDER ACT 1998

Introduced Drug Treatment and Testing Orders into the sentencing regime.

CRIMINAL JUSTICE AND COURT SERVICES ACT 2000

Created the power for certain suspects or defendants to be drug tested at virtually every stage in the criminal justice process, including the drug testing of prisoners released on parole. Also, this statute introduced Drug Abstinence Orders as part of the sentencing regime in respect of specified Class A drugs.

CRIMINAL JUSTICE AND POLICE ACT 2001

Intended to widen the scope of section 8 of the Misuse of Drugs Act (the offence of permitting/suffering drug offences on premises), but never put into force. This statute also enabled the courts to impose travel restriction orders on convicted drug traffickers.

PROCEEDS OF CRIME ACT 2002

Repeals the Drug Trafficking Act and restates the law on the proceeds of criminal conduct, including drug trafficking.

CRIMINAL JUSTICE ACT 2003

Makes possession of cannabis or cannabis resin arrestable offences (to coincide with the downgrading of cannabis from Class B to Class C). Increases the maximum penalties for the unlawful supply, possession with intent to supply, production, import/export and other offences connected with Class C drugs from 5 to 14 years. Lowers the minimum age to14 years regarding police power to drug test charged suspects, pre-sentence drug testing by the courts, and drug testing requirement when released on parole. Empowers the courts to impose a drug rehabilitation requirement, which includes drug treatment and testing, as part of a community order or suspended sentence order. Also, the courts may impose a drug treatment and testing requirement
within Action Plan Orders or Supervision Orders. Defendants who misuse drugs will be subject to a condition of bail that compels them to undergo assessment and follow-up treatment. Bail will be denied to those who refuse any of these conditions. Cases involving the unlawful import/export or production of Class A drugs are among those offences that can be retried.

ANTI-SOCIAL BEHAVIOUR ACT 2003

Part 1 gives the police and the courts a new power to close premises where Class A controlled drugs are being used, produced or supplied *and* where this is also causing serious public disruption.

DRUGS ACT 2005

Creates a duty on the courts to impose stiffer sentences on persons who deal in drugs in the vicinity of schools. The same applies where persons use young people as couriers for drugs or drug-related proceeds. The courts will also be given the power to presume that a person possessed drugs with intent to supply them if more than a certain amount of drugs are in their possession. (although the implementation of this provision has been postponed indefinitely). The police will have to obtain a suspect's consent before an intimate search for Class A drugs is carried out. Adverse inferences may be drawn if there is a refusal. Where a suspect swallows drugs the police may authorise an X-ray and/or an ultrasound scan but only with the suspect's consent. If refused, adverse inferences may also be drawn. Magistrates may authorise the police to detain arrested drug dealers for up to 192 hours where they have swallowed wrapped drugs (this is a power already held by customs officers that has been extended to the police). The police power to test suspects charged with an offence, for specified Class A drugs, has been extended to include testing on arrest. A discretionary power has been given to the police enabling them to require persons tested positive for specified Class A drugs, to attend drug assessments of their drug misuse; a follow-up assessment will be included where appropriate. The Drugs Act also introduces 'intervention orders' that run alongside anti-social behaviour orders where the conduct is caused by drug misuse. The 'magic mushroom' has been made a Class A substance in addition to the drug psilocin that is contained within this fungus. The controversial amendment made to section 8 of the Misuse of Drugs Act 1971 (permitting or suffering drug activities on premises), has been repealed by the Drugs Act 2005 before it was put into force.

Appendix 3: Overview of the Misuse of Drugs Act 1971

The institution of the Advisory Council on the Misuse of Drugs (section 1 and Schedule 1).

The classification of controlled drugs into three classes A, B and C, the meaning of certain technical expressions under the Act, and the changing of these classifications and definitions by means of Orders in Council (section 2 and Schedule 2).

The restriction on the importation and exportation of controlled drugs (section 3).

The restriction on the production and supply of controlled drugs (section 4)

The restriction on the possession of controlled drugs, and possession with intent to supply (section 5).

The restriction on the cultivation of the cannabis plant (section 6).

The power of the Home Secretary to make regulations in order to modify certain aspects of the Misuse of Drugs Act (sections 7, 10, 22 and 31).

The offence of permitting or suffering drug offences on premises (section 8).

The offences of smoking or otherwise using prepared opium, frequenting opium dens, or possessing equipment used or intended for opium smoking or the preparation of opium for smoking (section 9).

Prohibition of the supply etc. of articles for administering or preparing controlled drugs (drug paraphernalia)(section 9A).

The power of the Home Secretary to direct special precautions for the safe custody of controlled drugs to be taken at certain premises (section 11).

The power of the Home Secretary to give directions prohibiting practitioners and pharmacists convicted of certain offences etc. from prescribing or supplying controlled drugs; investigations into the latter and temporary directions (sections 12, 13, 14 , 15 and 16).

The power of the Home Secretary to demand information from doctors and pharmacists regarding upsurge in drug misuse within their areas (section 17).

Miscellaneous offences (including licence contravention and false statements to obtain a licence)(section 18).

Incitement to commit a drug offence (section 19).

Assisting in or inducing the commission outside the United Kingdom of a drug offence punishable under a corresponding law (sections 20 and 36).

Drug offences by corporations (section 21).

Police powers to search for controlled drugs and to obtain search warrants (section 23).

The penalties for drug offences (section 25 and Schedule 4)

Forfeiture of articles used in drug offences (section 27).

Proof of lack of knowledge etc. to be a defence to certain drug offences (section 28).

Service of documents (section 29).

Conditions and fees attached to licences and authorities (section 30).

Provision enabling the Home Secretary to promote research into controlled drugs (section 32).

Note that sections 24, 26, 33 and 34 have been repealed.

Appendix 4: Maximum Penalties for Drug Offences

Offence	Mode of Trial	Class A	Class B	Class C
Possession	S	12 months/ £5,000 fine	12 months/ £2,500 fine	12 months/ £1,000 fine
Possession	I	7 years/ unlimited fine	5 years/ unlimited fine	2 years/ unlimited fine
Possession with intent to supply	S	12 months/ £5,000 fine	12 months/ £5,000 fine	12 months/ £2,500 fine
Possession with intent to supply	I	Life/ unlimited fine	14 years/ unlimited fine	14 years/ unlimited fine
Supply	S	12 months/ £5,000 fine	12 months/ £5,000 fine	12 months/ £2,500 fine
Supply	I	Life/ unlimited fine	14 years/ unlimited fine	14 years/ unlimited fine
Production	S	12 months/ £5,000 fine	12 months/ £5,000 fine	12 months/ £2,500 fine
Production	I	Life/ unlimited fine	14 years/ unlimited fine	14 years/ unlimited fine
Occupier/manager permitting etc. on premises	S	12 months/ £5,000 fine	12 months/ £5,000 fine	12 months/ £2,500 fine
Occupier/manager permitting etc. on premises	I	14 years/ unlimited fine	14 years/ unlimited fine	14 years/ unlimited fine
Smuggling	S	12 months/ £5,000 fine	12 months/ £5,000 fine	12 months/ £5,000 fine
Smuggling	I	Life/ unlimited fine	14 years/ unlimited fine	14 years/ unlimited fine
Cultivation of cannabis plant	(S)	12 months/£5,000 fine (I) 14 years/unlimited fine		
Supplying articles	(S)	51 weeks/£5,000 fine		

NOTE: The maximum custodial sentences of 12 months (or 51 weeks) are due to come into force during 2007. Meanwhile, when tried summarily, all Class C offences and Class B possession attract a maximum of three months and all other offences a maximum of six months.

Appendix 5: Misuse of Drugs Regulations 2001

Schedule 1

Sixty named substances fall under Schedule 1. Nearly all are Class A (one is under Class B and five are under Class C). All controlled drugs under Schedule 1 are non-therapeutic and must not be prescribed to any patient. These drugs are therefore subject to the strictest controls, and a Home Office licence is required in order to lawfully produce, supply or possess any of them. On 18 July 2005, magic mushrooms were placed under Schedule 1 (as well as Class A). Under Regulation 4A to the Misuse of Drugs Regulations 2001, landowners or occupiers are not in unlawful possession of magic mushrooms where they are growing wild and uncultivated on their land. They are also legally protected where they take possession of these fungi when in the process of destroying or surrendering them.

Schedule 2

There are 119 named substances included under Schedule 2. About 80 per cent are Class A controlled drugs, approximately 18 per cent are Class B and about 2 per cent are Class C.

PERSONS LAWFULLY ENTITLED TO POSSESS AND SUPPLY SCHEDULE 2 CONTROLLED DRUGS

(1) a practitioner (meaning a doctor, dentist or veterinary surgeon);

(2) a pharmacist;

(3) a person lawfully conducting a retail pharmacy;

(4) a person in charge or acting person in charge of a hospital or nursing home which is wholly or mainly maintained by a public authority out of public funds or by charity or by voluntary subscriptions.

(5) in the case of such a drug supplied to her by a person responsible for the dispensing and supply of medicines at the hospital or nursing home, the sister or acting sister for the time being in charge of a ward, theatre, or other department in such a hospital or nursing home as aforesaid;

(6) a person who is in charge of a laboratory the recognised activities of which consist in, or include, the conduct of scientific education or research and which is attached to a university, university college or such a hospital as aforesaid or to any other institution approved for the purpose under this sub-paragraph by the Secretary of State;

(7) a public analyst appointed under section 27 of the Food Safety Act 1990;

(8) a sampling officer within the meaning of schedule 3 to the Medicines Act 1968;

(9) a person employed or engaged in connection with a scheme for testing the quality or amount of the drugs, preparations and appliances supplied under the National Health Service Act 1977 or the National Health Service (Scotland) Act 1978 and the regulations made thereunder;

(10) a person authorised by the Pharmaceutical Society of Great Britain for the purposes of section 108 or 109 of the Medicines Act 1968;

(11) persons who are members of an authorised group who are acting in accordance with their group authority;

(12) managers of ships and offshore installations where no doctor is present;

(13) midwives (who may possess and supply any controlled drug which is a medicine under the Medicines Act 1968);

(14) persons licensed under the Wildlife and Countryside Act 1981 to stupefy wild birds etc.;

(15) nurses under 'patient group directions' may possess and administer diamorphine but only to treat cardiac pain in accident and emergency departments or coronary care units in hospitals;

(16) nurses, registered midwives and pharmacists, trained as 'supplementary prescribers' may prescribe any schedule 2 drug to individual patients under a clinical management plan;

(17) 'Nurse Independent Prescribers' may prescribe oxycodone, diamorphine, morphine (or fentanyl for transdermal use), for use in palliative care; also diamorphine or morphine in respect of myocardial infarction or for severe pain relief after trauma or surgery.

Schedule 3

Eighteen named controlled drugs fall under this schedule. Approximately 90 per cent are Class C and about 10 per cent are Class B.

PERSONS LAWFULLY ENTITLED TO POSSESS AND SUPPLY SCHEDULE 3 CONTROLLED DRUGS

(1) a practitioner;

(2) a pharmacist;

(3) a person lawfully conducting a retail pharmacy;

(4) a person in charge of a laboratory the recognised activities of which consist in, or include, the conduct of scientific education or research;

(5) a public analyst appointed under section 27 of the Food Safety Act 1990;

(6) a sampling officer within the meaning of schedule 3 to the Medicines Act 1968;

(7) a person employed or engaged in connection with a scheme for testing the quality or amount of the drugs, preparations and appliances supplied under the National Health

Service Act 1977 or the National Health Service (Scotland) Act 1978 and the regulations made thereunder;

(8) a person authorised by the Pharmaceutical Society of Great Britain for the purposes of section 108 or 109 of the Medicines Act 1968;

(9) persons in charge of laboratories using any schedule 3 drug in chemical analysis as a buffering agent. This class of persons may also supply or offer to supply such drugs for the same purposes;

(10) persons in charge (or acting persons in charge) of a hospital or nursing home);

(11) sisters, or acting sisters, in charge of a ward, theatre, or other department of a hospital or nursing home who have been supplied schedule 3 drugs by a person responsible for dispensing and supplying medicines at such an establishment;

(12) persons licensed under the Wildlife and Countryside Act 1981 to stupefy wild birds etc;

(13) managers of ships and offshore installations where no doctor is present;

(14) midwives (who may possess or supply any controlled drug which is a medicine under the Medicines Act 1968);

(15) persons who are members of an authorised group who are acting in accordance with their group authority;

(16) nurses, registered midwives and pharmacists, trained as 'supplementary prescribers' may prescribe any schedule 3 drug to individual patients under a clinical management plan;

(17) 'Nurse Independent Prescribers' may prescribe buprenorphine for transdermal use in palliative care.

Schedule 4

Schedule 4 is divided into Parts 1 and 2. Those drugs under Part 1 (listed also in paragraph 1(a) under Class C) consist of 43 named substances that are mainly benzodiazepines and are subject to stricter controls compared to those under Part 2 (listed also in paragraph 1(b) under Class C) that are 58 named anabolic/androgenic steroids and growth hormones. The legal rules regarding the possession and supply of drugs falling under Part 1 of Schedule 4, are almost the same as those applicable to Schedule 3 controlled drugs. Nurse Independent Prescribers may prescribe diazepam, lorazepam and midazolam in palliative care and treatment for epilepsy, and chlordiazepoxide hydrochloride and diazepam for treatment of alcoholism; and under Patient Group Directions, nurses, paramedics, health visitors, midwives, ophthalmic opticians, chiropodists, orthoptists, physiotherapists, radiographers ,occupational therapists, orthotists and prosthetists may administer any Part 1 Schedule 4 drug, except in injectable form to treat addicts. Also, specially trained nurses, registered midwives and pharmacists ('supplementary prescribers') may prescribe to individual patients any Schedule 4 drug under a clinical management plan. The supply of drugs that are listed under Part 2 of Schedule 4, are subject also to nearly the same restrictions as those which apply to Schedule 3. However, anyone may lawfully possess a Part 2 Schedule 4 drug provided it is in the form of a medicinal product. Otherwise, the rules applicable to Schedule 3 drugs will apply.

Schedule 5

These are medicines that contain controlled drugs in such small quantities, and/or prepared in such a manner as to make their extraction so difficult, that anyone may possess them. Nurse Independent Prescribers may prescribed codeine phosphate, dihydrocodeine tartrate and co-phenotrope. Under Patient Group Directions, nurses, paramedics, health visitors, midwives, ophthalmic opticians, chiropodists, orthoptists, physiotherapists, radiographers, occupational therapists, orthotists and prosthetists may administer any Schedule 5 drug. Supplementary prescribers may prescribe any Schedule 5 drug to individual patients under a clinical management plan.

Index

Visit **www.watersidepress.co.uk** for a wide range of books on **Crime and Punishment**
including
Drug Trafficking and Criminal Policy
Drug Treatment in Prison
Women, Drugs and Custody
Drugs, Victims and Race

Covert Human Intelligence Sources
The 'Unlovely' Face of Police Work
~ Roger Billingsley (Ed.)
Foreword John Grieve QPM and Jon Murphy

A unique insight into the until now hidden **world of police informers** and associated forms of covert human intelligence.

Edited by the head of the Covert Policing Standards Unit at New Scotland Yard, this book is the first to look **behind the scenes of undercover police work** since the authorities decided that aspects of a non-sensitive nature should no longer be kept secret.

Covert Human Intelligence Sources **includes an Introduction plus**

- Defence Perspective
- Regulation of CHIS
- Immunity from the Law
- Assisting Offenders
- Management of Information from the Public
- Juvenile Informers
- European Perspective
- Debriefing A New Way forward?
- Risk Management
- The Informer Relationship

Covert Human Intelligence Sources contains contributions from a range of disciplines and field of study, including senior police officers, lawyers and academic commentators.

Oct 2008 | Paperback | ISBN 978-1-904380-44-3

Police and Policing
An Introduction ~ Peter Villiers

Well-known former Bramshill Police College tutor **Peter Villiers** explains the role of the police from their Victorian origins to the local police forces and nationwide police organizations of the present day. Includes notes on the role of the Home Secretary in relation to law and order and public safety as well as a **Glossary** of 'policespeak' and a timeline spanning more than 200 years to the present day. An ideal introduction.

Jan 2009 | 160 pages | Paperback | ISBN 978-1-904380-46-7

The New Home Office
An Introduction
~ Bryan Gibson Foreword David Faulkner

This timely publication explains the duties and responsibilities of the Home Office following its reorganization in 2007.

The New Home Office provides an accessible introduction but with sufficient detail for the more critical reader seeking to understand both the historic and modern-day role of this key office of State. Easy to read - written in the style of the acclaimed Waterside Press Introductory Series - this handbook contains a wealth of information making it an indispensable resource. An ideal text for students and practitioners alike.

A closely observed account of the 21st century arrangements to ensure public safety, law enforcement and crime reduction in the UK that can be read on its own or alongside *The Ministry of Justice: An Introduction* and *The Criminal Justice System: An Introduction*.

Reviews of the First Edition (with *The New Ministry of Justice*)

- 'Should be read by everybody involved in the Criminal Justice System': *Internet Law Book Reviews*
- 'Invaluable': *Thames View*
- 'Bryan Gibson and Waterside Press are to be congratulated on producing these stimulating books': *Justice of the Peace*

The contents of *The New Home Office* include:

- A Basic Overview
- Public Safety, Liberty and Protecting the Public
- The Police and Policing
- Crime Prevention and Crime Reduction
- Terrorism and Emergency Powers
- Border Controls, Immigration and Asylum
- Safeguarding Personal Identity
- A Note of the Department's Extensive Miscellaneous Responsibilities
- The Changed Role of the Home Secretary

2nd Edition | July 2008 | 172 pages | Paperback | ISBN 978-1-904380-49-8

❈ WATERSIDE PRESS

The Criminal Justice System
An Introduction
~ Bryan Gibson and Paul Cavadino

A comprehensive and accessible overview of the CJS, its framework, institutions, practitioners and working methods—that will be of interest to readers seeking an up-to-date description of this important sphere of public life.

An informative, practical handbook which describes the wide-ranging developments and changes that have taken place in relation to crime prevention, public safety and the punishment of offenders.

- Investigation, arrest and charge
- The police and policing
- The Crown Prosecution Service
- The courts of law
- Trial and sentence
- Appeal and review
- Due process
- Judges and magistrates
- Law officers
- The Criminal Defence Service
- Advocates and legal representation
- Victims and witnesses
- The Youth Justice System
- The Probation Service
- HM Prison Service
- Imprisonment and parole
- Independent Monitoring Board

- The private sector
- The voluntary sector
- Strategy
- Criminal policy
- Cabinet committees
- Partnership and working together
- Community justice
- Restorative justice
- Constitutional affairs and human rights
- Interpreters
- Accountability, oversight, inspection and monitoring
- Guidelines, codes, protocols and Best Practice.

- *Plus* - now includes a **Glossary of Words, Phrases, Acronyms and Abbreviations**

Highly acclaimed since first published in 1995, *The Criminal Justice System* covers the entire spectrum of the criminal process against a backdrop of the Common Law, legislation and human rights—from investigation and arrest to trial, sentence, release from prison and parole, as well as key modern-day reforms such as the **Ministry of Justice** and new-style **Home Office**.

3rd Edition | June 2008 | 240 pages | ISBN 978-1-904380-43-6

☷ WATERSIDE PRESS